Lexi Wright

Starting Things Off Wright

An Autobiography

By Lexi Wright

Lexi Wright

Starting Things Off Wright

"Life is what you make it, so start things of right, and make it what you want."

- Lexi Wright

Lexi Wright

For my family, Thanks for making life the best.

And dedicated to James Hetfield, who inspired me to rock!

Starting Things Off Wright

INTRODUCTION

To become a great guitar player is as easy as acing the
ACT's. It takes heart and effort put into time and control of
what you are learning. Even though most guitar players
expect to be super great when they first pick up the guitar
then find out it takes time to be the best. Time is defined as
effort and sweat and blood. You got to practice till you
sweat and bleed from your fingers while you play the notes
on the fretboard. It is relatively easy to play the guitar, it
just takes time. There are a million things in the world
people have talent for, or so-called talent. Talent is just the
result of practicing and playing for years on end. If talent
was being great, then wouldn't you be a pro as soon as you
touch the guitar? Most famous guitar players in the world
were born in a rich family where they could get guitar
lessons and become a pro by age 9 or younger. Even if you
are poor, you can still become great, it just takes time. Most
of the time, when people first pick up the guitar, they pluck
the strings and try to play the notes on the fretboard and
'oh, well, it's too hard', then they put it down and never
touch it again. They lose interest and find something 'easy'
to do. If playing guitar was easy, then everyone would play.
You have to have interest. But even interest can make it
hard to play. Don't give up. Keep playing. Even if you sweat

Lexi Wright

and bleed till your bones in your fingers start showing, that's good! Keep playing. This book is about how I became great, from horribly bad, to a guitar legend!

Most bands fall apart because of the guitar being 'too hard to play'. If you want to be great, start things off Wright and learn. Sweat. Bleed. TAKE TIME. Remember, *LSB, Learn, Sweat, Bleed*. Also, it doesn't depend on what style of music you want to major in, be it metal, country, pop, whatever. You still have to *LSB*. Practice makes perfect and perfect makes you great, and being great makes you a legend, and being a legend means being a legendary icon forever. I am not going to teach you how to play the guitar or how to read music; you have to do that on your own. Do whatever it takes to practice till you bleed. Shed your skin, let the bones show through, that just means you're determined. Anyways, this book is a biography, not a teaching book or whatever. This is just telling you about my life and how I became what I am today. Hope you enjoy this book and you can take from me and learn from my mistakes and learn from my successes.

Lexi Wright

Contents

Lexi Wright

1 | The Life Left Behind

Being the first child born in 1999 was new to my parents. I was their first child. January is a cold month to be born in. The time it took to birth me was endless, seemed like it took forever for me to decide to come out into the world. Nearly born on the 15th because I took so long. But since I was born at 11:57pm, my birthday is on the 14th. When my parents noticed I was a female, they gave me my name, Madison Sack. That has been my name for years. When my brothers joined me in 2000 and 2002, I had someone to enjoy life with and share life with. My parents were the most amazing parents ever. They always hung out with us and gave us equal time though there were three of us. Mom worked while dad would play with us. One thing I think is interesting is, dad took me to the store to pick out a toy. He thought I'd choose a *Barbie*, but instead I chose a little blue *Chevy* model pickup truck. I guess I was always like this, a tomboy. Even as a little kid, I liked boy things. I remember driving my little *Volkswagen* around the driveway thinking I was all big shot. "I want to go to the store and buy chicken nuggets." I told my mom one day. I drove my *Volkswagen* to the stop sign while my mom walked beside me. Dad was an amazing guitar player; I

Lexi Wright

remember him playing '*Sweet Child 'O Mine*' by *Guns N' Roses* while my brothers and I would dance around playfully. We loved it when dad played guitar. I remember mom and dad both could recite the '*Cat in the Hat*' because I loved that book so much. They let me read it one day and I read it like a pro, they thought I just remembered the words, so they gave me a harder book, I read it with ease. They were impressed that their 3-year-old daughter was reading.

The first 3 years of my life was awesome, until it all got ruined by three people. My grandmother was one of them. My dad's mom to be exact. Let's just say she was a bitch. A total witch. She could not stand my parents having a daughter; she wanted me as her own. So, she stole me. Made up lies to CPS and got custody of me. Her plan was that I was going to be her little sidekick and never leave her side until I turned 18. She made it so my brothers could stay with her, too. Put a restraining order on my parents and kicked them out of the house so they could not see us. I remember this one day, I saw mom and dad parked outside, so I told William and Dillon, 'mommy and daddy are outside!' and we ran outside the house with excitement to see mom and dad. Our grandma tried to stop us but she couldn't. "Get back here!" She yelled. William and Dillon stopped, unsure what to do. But I kept running, into mom's

Starting Things Off Wright

arms hanging out of her car window. I stopped ten feet in front of her. "We'll get you guys back, I promise." Mom told me. I looked into her eyes and saw the truth. She knew she'd get us back. Away from my grandma's evil hands. Well, being treated with hate and unusual parenting, we didn't know how to act. My grandma taught me to act like a bitch, hit my brothers for no reason and it being their fault that I hit them for some reason. She would see me do bad and reward me with good. I was 4 and this went on till I was 9. I had to take care of my brothers at age 5 because all my grandma did was sit on her laptop and talk to guys on *Myspace* while my grandpa worked. If she was not on her laptop, she was sleeping, so she never fed us. She hardly ever came out of her room. I was making peanut butter and jelly sandwiches for my brothers and made such a big mess trying to figure out how to make these sandwiches at age 4, 5, and 6. By the time I reached age six, I would throw tantrums until I got what I wanted. I never heard the word 'no'. My brothers were treated like shit. They were just 'playmates'. I was the 'princess'. If my grandma got out of bed, it was to drive the van to *McDonald's* which was right at the bottom of the hill in Reading, Ohio. If not *McDonald's*, then *Burger King*, or *Rally's*. We ate at those restaurants every once in a while, for breakfast, lunch, and dinner if we ran out of food at home. We never really had a

Lexi Wright

real meal. At night, when we would be put to bed in the basement, I would sometimes lay awake at night, remembering mom saying she'd get us back. Even though I didn't understand what was happening to us, I still couldn't wait for mom and dad to be our real parents again. Things would be better when they get us back. All those years of being transformed from an innocent little girl, to a witch was bad. I could not go to school because the teachers would give me work to do and I would rip it up and throw fits. Because I didn't want to do the work. I was thrown around school after school, each being for behavior problems. I was also put on medication for my behavior. So many pills to take. You name the anti-depressant; I was on it. I remember my grandma let my parents stay at the house to clean, and mom had to force the medicine down my throat. She was sad to see what happened to her daughter, but she had no idea how to fix it.

My mom and grandma fought every time she let them stay, and then kick them out again. When mom told nana, that's what we called her, that she wanted us back, nana took me with her to Florida. She only met this guy on *Myspace* the night before. My grandparents divorced, and nana took me with her on her journey to meet this guy. I was only 7. Not knowing anything, I enjoyed the ride. But when we arrived and I saw this guy, I was immediately

Starting Things Off Wright

scared. Something about him scared me bad. That night, when it was time to go to bed, they gave me a huge bed, turned out the lights and left the room. As they guy left, I never knew his name, I saw a huge knife in his back pocket, which scared me terribly. I snuck out of my room and told nana about his knife, and she ignored me, acted like I was stupid. "Ok, go to bed. You're just scared because we moved." No, I was afraid of some random dude with a ten-inch blade in his back pocket. I went back to my room and hid under the covers until I got brave and fell asleep. The next day, nana took me to the beach. I never saw the ocean before. I got in the water, and I saw seaweed floating in the water. But being 7, I thought it was a shark. I screamed and ran out of the water. Nana pulled seaweed off my back and showed it to me. "It's just seaweed, stop acting like that." She said, as she whizzed the seaweed back into the water. I grabbed my bucket and shovel and tried to make a sandcastle, but the water kept washing it away. I got mad and threw my bucket into the water. But I was too afraid to get it back. We finally left and we stopped by a souvenir shop next to the beach. Nana bought me *Shark Fin Soup* and I tried it. It was very salty and fishy; I spit it out.

Lexi Wright

When we got back to the house, we watched *Jaws*. Just the movie to watch right after getting scared an hour ago, right? After the movie, we ate again. Seemed like all we did was watch movies and eat. "I prepared this meat for you." The guy said. He had a plate of meat with blood leaking from it. "It's not cooked, but I'll cook it for you." He spoke. Nana went into the living room and got on her laptop as she sat on the couch. The guy walks in after twenty minutes or so, and noticed nana on her laptop. "Who are you talking too?" I guess he saw the *Myspace* page. "Nobody." Nana panicked. I just stood in the kitchen watching from behind the wall as they fought. After a while, the guy walked out of the house. I was scared so bad, that I went to my room and saw a cabinet that had a sign on it that read, "TOOLS", so I opened it. There were so many tools, but very organized. I looked through the cabinet and found a hammer. I picked up the hammer and ran out of my room. I held it over my grandma's head and threatened to throw it at her. "I want mommy!" I screamed, as I dropped the hammer behind me. Nana fumbled for her phone and called my mom. So, I went back to my room and packed and waited to get in the van. Turns out we didn't leave that day; we left the next day. When we finally left, I was filled with excitement. Mom, dad, and Aunt Kate, nana's sister who was also in on this whole thing, all met up with us at a hotel in Georgia. Mom hugged me so tight, I couldn't breathe. She was so glad to see me. Dad was talking to Kate and nana and mom was talking to me. "We hardly ever slept these past three days." She spoke. Her eyes had bags under them, so I knew she didn't sleep well. "We prayed every night that you would be okay. I'm glad you're back, because we cried ourselves to sleep each night." They did not trust this guy nana was with. Neither did I. Dad got back in the car with Kate and drove back home. Kate was mad because part of their plan was ruined. Mom and dad were so happy to have me back.

When we got back into our state, Ohio, we stopped to get gas. The gas station we went to was right in Sharonville, next to Evandale, so Kate got out and walked home. We filled our tank and drove home. My brothers were outside playing while my grandpa was inside trying to go through his bills. When we got inside, I felt okay again. My brothers ran up to me and hugged me. "We missed you, Madison." Dillon said. Pawpaw, that's what we call our grandpa, called my parents in the room. "You guys are going to have to move out, I can't afford to pay rent. After Leslie left, I can't afford this. I'm sorry, I wouldn't do this if I didn't have to. The electric is being shut off--." In mid-sentence, the power went out. Mom and dad went down to the basement and I followed, scared. I was easily frightened, I guess. "Mommy, what's happening?" I asked. My brothers came downstairs,

Lexi Wright

too. "Well, since we're all down here, let's start packing and cleaning." Mom said. I guess she didn't hear me. Dad rented a dumpster and we carried garbage out to it. Everything that was going with us got put into boxes, anything that wasn't got thrown out. I remember this big white *Winnie-the-pooh* bear with a blue nose and blue shirt. I loved it. But I had to throw him out because there was not enough room for him to go. I still had my little *pooh*. He's been with me ever since I was 3. We finally got everything done and we headed out, in search of a new home. We went over to the library and mom and dad looked for a new place. After about an hour, they finally found something. A three-bedroom apartment in Felicity, Ohio. We headed to our new place. After a while of driving and getting lost, we found someone that was heading to Felicity. "We never been out here before, we're from the city, do you know how to get to Felicity?" Dad asked. "Oh sure! We were just heading there." They spoke. We followed them. We finally found the apartments that mom and dad were looking at the day before. We moved in and lived there for only a year. I was 10 here. Mom and dad had custody of us again, and they got my behavior under control, got me off the medicine. We moved to a trailer here in Felicity, and we've lived here since. We lived in Felicity for 8 years and counting. It's a small town with NO stoplights, only stop

Starting Things Off Wright

signs. Only about 0.5 miles long either way you go, and farms on every road out of Felicity. 133, 222, and 756 are the roads out or in. We have a library, two gas stations, two stores, two restaurants, and a building that keeps changing to different things every year, and two bars, and one post office, and one bank, a police department, a fire/ambulance department, and 4 churches. For a small town, that's a lot of places. We can walk to any of these places. The main road, North Market Street, which is also 133/222, separates north and south of Felicity. We live on the south side and never really go on the north side, most of the punks live there. There's no law against us going over there, we just don't want to deal with the punks. The cops are so crooked, you can "work for them" and not get in trouble at all. Even if it's so illegal you would be in prison, they wouldn't arrest you because you're "working for them".

By the time I reached 13, I've gotten to know life pretty well. My dad loved to hit the trails at *East Fork State Park* and ride his mountain bike through the woods. He would take one of us at a time, so he could make sure we stay with him and not get lost through the woods, or hurt by falling off the edge. He also liked to hunt with William. They used to go to *East Fork* to hunt, just for fun. They were trying to find woodchucks, but never had any luck. We would swim in the lake at *East Fork* as well. But after

Lexi Wright

learning that the lake was harmful to swim in, we never even went near it. But back to the trails, dad loved to ride through the woods. "I used to ride my bike through the woods all the time when I was a kid." He spoke. Dad has done a lot in his childhood, even though his mom completely hated him, that's why she took me. I'd always volunteer to go ride with him because I loved it. We would hit the beginner trail first to get warmed up, which is relatively easy to ride, just a couple obstacles like bridges, hills, and roots we have to watch out for. The first time I rode the trail, I was too scared to ride across the bridge, which is only about 2 feet off the ground if that. It's supposed to take you an hour to get through the trail, but it usually takes us about two, because dad would fly through then wait for us on top off a hill, then we'd go again. We'd take drink breaks to. Water. We always had water, never pop, or anything unhealthy. I love my dad; he is so fun to hang out with. I get mad sometimes and say I hate him, but I don't mean it, I'm just angry at the moment. Anyways, sometimes dad would get us up at 6 am and feed us omelets and we'd go hiking through the woods. Dad loved being in the woods, he said it reminded him of home. I enjoyed it too, but would get mad because my knees would start hurting. Mom was working at *Subway* in Bethel at this time.

2 | The Start of Terror

During the summer of me being 13, now this part gets sad, I made a friend. (I'm not going to name her out of due respect of her privacy.) She had just moved to the neighborhood and was playing outside by herself. She was tossing a ball over the wires between the telephone poles in front of her house. I went over and said hello. (I never had a friend before; this is my first friend.) I was shy. "Can I play?" I asked. "Sure." She spoke. We played *Throw the Ball Over the Wire* for hours, till she got tired of it. "What's your name?" She asked. "Madison." I replied. (It was actually switched, but remember, I'm not naming her) We talked and introduced ourselves to each other's family. I was happy to have a friend. The next day, when school let out, I went over to her house, right across the street, and waited for her to come down the street. She is 2 years younger than me. "Hey, want to play?" I'd ask. "I guess." She was texting on her phone. Her mom worked every weekday, from 5 am to 4pm. And she had no dad. She was home alone for a while. I would try to hang out with her every day. This went on for one whole year, until she got tired of me. She had made much more friends since she moved here. She'd be with her group of friends when I'd ask her to play. "No, are you retarded?" Her friends laughed. I just stood there,

Lexi Wright

unsure how to feel. "Uh............." I never could think of any comebacks. She started being really mean to me. Once, she asked me to walk up to the pop machine with her when she was alone. So, I did. When we got about 20 feet away from it, she hands me a dollar and says to get two cans. I did. I turned around to give her her cans of pop, but she was walking away talking to some boy. I walked home, slowly, very sad. When I got home, I didn't drink those pops, I gave them to my brothers. This whole, ditching me, bullying me, went on for 3 years. I finally was able to get back in regular school. I went to the library in school and got pushed down. I look and there she is, picking one of my assignments off the ground and ripping it. "Why?" I asked. And it wasn't just her, it was the whole high school. Yes, I'm 16 here. She spread rumors about me, that I did bad things to boys and was a horrible person. All the kids would make fun of me and pick on me. I never talked to anyone, I stayed far away from people as possible. I'd go to class and sit in the farthest chair from people as possible. I was very quiet, I never spoke. Do my work, don't speak. One day in Choir, while we waited for our teacher to come in, this one boy asked me if I had sex with boys. "No. That's gross." He walked away. I thought sex was gross in these years. The next day, when I came into Choir, nobody was there. But on the whiteboard, someone wrote, 'Madison is the ugliest, smelliest, stupidest person ever, she should kill herself.' I believed those words. I stared at the words as they repeated over and over in my head. I felt a tap on my shoulder so I turn around and the whole class is there now. Somehow, they all just appeared. I took my place and just stood there. The teacher came in. She didn't know us by name yet, so when she saw the whiteboard, she just erased it without asking questions. I started skipping classes, refusing lunch, and hiding in the bathroom. One day, I brought a knife to school. I was going to cut myself when I hid in the bathroom, but the teacher saw it and reported me to the principle. I got suspended.

I've come to realize that she is sleeping with the whole town. That's why she's so 'cool'. Me, I don't, so I'm the one to bully. One day, when she was walking home from school, (I was expelled) I stopped her. "Why are you being so mean to me?" No answer, she just throws a book in my face. It hurt so bad. I threw a punch and gave her a big black eye without even realizing I punched her until I saw her eye. She ran inside, crying. She called her mom home from work. Her mom was here so fast, (did she speed?) Her mom saw her black eye and told her to fight me again. Instead, she was texting on *Facebook*, saying 'I just beat up Madison'. When she wouldn't fight me, her mom called the

Lexi Wright

cops. I nearly got tazzed and was arrested for assault. We were never friends again. In 2016, it all FINALLY stopped.

3 | That's Interesting

Just like anyone else, I have many interests and inspirations. One person who I totally wanted to be like was *Carrie Underwood*. She was my inspirement to sing. I never had the courage to sing, even in front of my parents. I'd sing *Carrie Underwood*'s songs in my room and then try to get the courage to sing. When I finally did, I was in talent shows. I tried very hard to be just like her. The first talent show I ever did was at my church. *'Felicity Idol'* was the name of it. I sang *'Something in the Water'* and felt very nervous while singing, but when I got to the chorus, I felt great. The next year, I sang *'How Great Thou Art'* in *Carrie Underwood*'s version. I loved Country music at this time. (There's a video of this on my *Facebook* page) At my school, before I got expelled, they had a talent show called *'Dream Big'*. I sang *'Blown Away'*. Any talent show I could get on, I did. Never won any of them, but I enjoyed singing. This whole, listening to Country and singing *Carrie Underwood*'s songs went on till last year. Last year, 2016, I got introduced to *Metallica*. My taste immediately changed. Now, I listen to Heavy Metal. *Metallica* inspires me to play guitar and sing almost every day. I was interested in Country when I first started singing. A Country Artist is what I wanted to be. I loved to sing. My dad didn't like Country, he liked

Lexi Wright

Rock, same with most of my family, but mom liked Country, though. I got interested in drums and I wanted to be a drummer for a rock band. But when I saw how hard it was to play, I gave it up. I thought it was easy. What my biggest interest is, is singing. I want to sing. Now, I'm very interested in guitar. I've noticed how hard it is to play the guitar, but it's something I've decided I want to do. Sing and play Rhythm Guitar. I've started listening to rock and heavy metal. My most favorite band is *Metallica*. But I like other bands such as *Iron Maiden, Def Leppard, Slayer, Motley Crue*, Guns N' Roses, *Green Day*, and *Lynyrd Skynyrd*. I mostly listen to these bands and *102.7 WEBN* on the radio, but I also listen to *Carrie Underwood* since she is my biggest inspiration. Before the interest of singing or playing any instrument ever came about, I had the interest of magic. I did card tricks and tried to read people's minds. During one of my practices of another trick in my room, I found my calling while listening to *Carrie Underwood* and other Country Artists on *b105.1*. Singing. Magic was my most favorite thing to do in 2012 and I thought I'd do big shows like all the famous magicians. I ended up disliking magic after a while, because it ended up getting really boring. Pulling off a card trick and guessing the right number every now and then is pretty cool, but I never was able to walk on water or actually fool someone. I don't have a talent for tricking someone. I dropped magic all together and started to sing. Each time I sang one of *Carrie Underwood*'s songs, I'd try to train my voice to match hers. I remember the first time I first tried to sing in front of my parents, dad and mom would stay up late and listen to rock music like *Guns N' Roses* or *Lynyrd Skynyrd* real loud, especially Friday nights, dad would get drunk and sing and I'd be up and walk in there. Dad would try to get me to sing with him, but I thought my voice sucked and I thought they'd laugh or tell me to shut up. (Dad finally gave up drinking and he doesn't really drink now.)

I'd write songs for my parents, like for their birthdays or their anniversary. Sometimes, I'd lie and say that I had to make a music video and write a song for school, (I was homeschooled in Ecot in 2012) so my dad would help me make a good video. I rewrote *Michael Jackson*'s song *'Beat It'* and called it *'Solve It'*. It was about doing hard homework. I tried to make a music video and record myself singing, but my parents would be around and I'd get really nervous. "If you can't sing in front of us, how are you going to sing in front of thousands of people?" Dad asked me. I stared at my paper of lyrics I had written down in case I forgot the words. "I don't know." Suddenly, I felt courage hit me. I sang the first verse and felt a wave of courage fill my body. My legs were shaking and I felt weak and very

Lexi Wright

much like throwing up at first, but after the burst of courage, it all changed. After recording the song, I looked at my parents and hoped they were proud, but dad was playing a video game and paused to say, ' good job' and mom was cooking, I liked the feeling of courage while I sang that song, so I tried my hand at writing my own songs. Not having any instruments or the know-how to play, I couldn't make my own music. I tried to download non-copyrighted music off *YouTube*, but you had to buy it and I didn't have any money, so my lyrics for my songs ended up getting thrown away in disappointment and sadness. In 2014, I borrowed my mom's laptop and did karaoke versions of *Carrie Underwood* songs and recorded myself. By this time, I had the courage of any rock star. I put my recordings of my covers on a CD. I thought the CD would make record producers want to put me in the spotlight. I listened to my CD in a CD player and realized it wasn't the gold I was looking for. I put the CD away and it's been there since 2014. A few months later, I dug my lyrics that I had written before out of the trash and sang them to myself. I thought, 'wow! This would be a hit!" So, I looked up non-copyrighted music on *YouTube* again and downloaded it then sang my songs (I found a way around paying for it). I recorded them and made another CD. Again, I listened to it in a CD player and, it sucked. I put it with my first CD. Ever

Starting Things Off Wright

since, I never recorded any songs. I'd still write songs every now and then, but I couldn't create my own music. In the summer of 2015, I discovered *America's Got Talent* on *YouTube* and I watched people sing, play instruments, do all kinds of acts. I wanted to get on that show. So, I had my dad record me singing 'Church Bells" by *Carrie Underwood* in 2016, when *America's Got Talent* came back for another season. I sent in the video and hoped for a response, never got one. Ever since I found this talent show on *YouTube*, it's been one of my biggest dreams to get on that show and win it. Sometimes dreams show up in unique places at unique times.

Above Lexi Wright plays guitar to "*St. Anger*" by *Metallica* (Picture used for *Facebook* Profile pic)

Lexi Wright

Above Lexi Wright plays *"Unforgiven I"* by *Metallica*

Above Lexi Wright plays *"One"* by *Metallica*

Starting Things Off Wright

Those are just a few pictures I've added. Since I've gotten interested in playing guitar, I've been playing for hours a day. I really enjoy it. It's something I really want to do. But like I was stating, my biggest interest is heavy metal. *Iron Maiden*'s songs, *"Fear of the Dark"*, *"Run to the Hills"*, *"Hallowed be Thy Name"*, and *"Two Minutes to Midnight"* have been some of the songs I listen to. Also, *"Raining Blood"* and *"Angel of Death"* by *Slayer*, *"Burnout"* by *Green Day*, *"Free Bird"*, *"Simple Man"*, *"Tuesday's Gone"*, and *"Sweet Home Alabama"* by *Lynyrd Skynyrd*, *"Girls, Girls, Girls"*, and *"The Dirt"* by *Motley Crue*, and *"Perfect"*, *"Welcome to my Life"*, and *"I'm Just a Kid"* by *Simple Plan* are some songs I've added to my playlist of the most awesome heavy metal songs. And I know, *Simple Plan* and *Lynyrd Skynyrd* are not heavy metal, but I still listen to them because I like rock. I've been diagnosed with Major Depression so when I listen to *Simple Plan* or watch depressing videos on *YouTube*, it's because I'm in that dark place of mind. Sometimes my depression causes me to act in a very mean manner and say things I don't mean. Sometimes during these dark times, I lose interest in guitar playing and gain interest in being alone in the dark while hiding in a very far away corner. It seems like every day I get like this, and I don't know why. Other times, I try so hard to be happy. It's hard to smile and be happy, because

Lexi Wright

I'm so down. My parents try to lift me up, but sometimes I yell at them or throw things. It could be the simplest thing, like taking a shower, and I get depressed. UGH, I wish I didn't have depression. My brothers have minor depression. And I'm not going to lie, there has been some suicidal attempts. I've tied a cord around my neck and jumped out the window, I've tied a rope around my neck and jumped off the branch of a tree outside, I've cut myself, but I never drank bleach. I fear death, and I fear dying. I have witnessed death once before and I don't want to be a part of it. No, it was not anyone in my family, it was a friend of ours. He nearly died from an overdose. STAY AWAY FROM DRUGS. But anyway, being a Christian, I've never successfully attempted suicide. I guess being treated like shit all your life can cause some mental damage in your brain. No lies are in this book, it's all honest statements. I do smoke weed. Relaxing and calming, yes, I enjoy it. Anyway, when I'm not down in the dumps, I play my guitar and sing. Singing is my passion, I love it. Playing guitar is my passion, I love it. Don't just listen to heavy metal, live it.

Starting Things Off Wright

4 | Pictures

Here are some pictures of my teenage life. From age 13 to 18.

Photos taken by me, Dillon Sack, Jennifer Sack, and Donald Sack III.

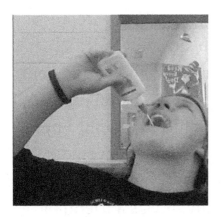

Above (Left) Lexi Wright drinks milk

from a glue bottle as a prank

Above (Right) Lexi Wright studies

music at home. Book borrowed from library.

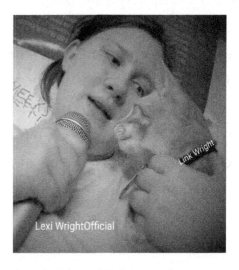

Above (Left) Lexi Wright poses

for picture

Above (Right) Lexi Wright sings to her cat,

Domenique, aka Link Wright

Lexi Wright

Above (Left) Lexi Wright hangs out with her cat

Above (Right) Lexi Wright shows off her

favorite album from *"Metallica"*

Above (Left) Lexi Wright poses

with her mom

Above (Right) A nice family meal

Starting Things Off Wright

Above (Left) Lexi Wright plays

"*Master of Puppets*" by *Metallica*

Above (Right) Lexi Wright turns 18

Above (Left) Lexi poses with her mom

Above (Right) Lexi poses with her dad in Downtown, Cincinnati

Lexi Wright

Above (Left) Lexi plays guitar

to "*One*" by *Metallica*

Above (Right) Lexi hangs out with her favorite singer,

James Hetfield from *Metallica* (a cardboard cutout she made)

Above (Left) Lexi rides her bike around town

Above (Right) Lexi plays "*For Whom the Bell*

Tolls" by *Metallica* for the first time

5 | PHA-Q

Yes, in the first chapter you've learned about my childhood and a little about my teenage life, but you don't know details that need to be known. Like, when exactly was I born? The 15th? The 14th? It was January, we know that, but what day? This chapter will explain those types of things.

It was 11:57pm at the hospital where I was born. So, it was three minutes to midnight, I was born January 14, 1999. And I don't believe in that transgender or choosing your own sex gig, that bullshit. You were either born a female or a male. There are not 5 genders, either, only 2. But now you're learning about my beliefs. I support Trump and like his idea of ending Abortion. Murder is wrong, it says so in the Bible. God put it as one of His rules, Ten Commandments. (I'm not exactly good at writing books. I can't do it. This book, it helps my future, so I'm writing it.) Ok. About Me. My name is Madison Sack. How is my name also Lexi Wright? "Lexi Wright" is a stage name. I came up with this name at home. At school, there were classmates with the name Lexi. I didn't know that when I came up with my name. My grandpa informed me that our family is related to the Wright Bros. so I wanted my last name to be "Wright". I couldn't find a name that fit with it. Eventually,

Lexi Wright

I found it on *"Google"* the name "Lexi". I put those two together, and it sounded great, to me at least. I loved the name. So, that's my stage name. As of this moment, as I'm writing this sentence right now, I am 18. It is 2017 right now. The month is March, three days until William turns 17. My eyes are blue, my hair, I like it short, and colored black and blue, but the natural color is brown. I am American. Born and raised American, I love my country. My favorite colors are black, blue, and red. I'm not a big fan of movies. But when I do watch movies, it's something like *Pulp Fiction*, the *Fast & Furious Series*, the *Twilight Series*, and my favorite movie, *Ace Ventura: Pet Detective*. My favorite song ever is *Fuel* by *Metallica*. My favorite *Carrie Underwood* song is *Forever Changed*. I was born in Cincinnati, Ohio.

More beliefs, be warned this may upset you. I believe that gay or homosexuality is wrong. I stand by my beliefs. God said in Leviticus 18:22- "You shall not lie with mankind as with womankind, it is an abomination to the Lord your God." Also, in Leviticus 20:13- "If a man has sexual relations with a man as one does with a woman, both of them have done what is detestable. They are to be put to death; their blood will be on their own heads." I believe in the Word of God. Jesus is the way, the truth, and the life. Money cannot buy happiness; Heaven is where happiness is. God is happiness and love. I do believe in ghosts. Why? Because I have witnessed some paranormal activity in my life. So has my dad. This part I do not like. It's opposite of my religion, but I'll include anyway. This is when I was 9. Our beds were in the basement of the house where we lived with our grandma. Turns out she did evil things. It was dark because it was bedtime. Dillon and I were the only ones awake. William fell asleep. Well, Dillon and I were talking about a clubhouse, like all kids do, and we were giving each other cool ideas. Suddenly it got hot in the room and I look and see the circle with a star in the middle in flames, the flames shoot up and back down, then gone. Nothing there except....... yes, he was there. I'm not lying. There's no way I can lie. The devil was red, but he didn't have hooves, he had a bunch of horns on his head, and giant claws. He had regular feet, but they looked mutilated. Glowing red eyes, and the sharpest teeth. He did have the pointy tail and pitchfork, but the pitchfork had flames on the top. He looked around then looked at me, growled softly, then vanished quickly when I screamed for mom. It was the scariest thing to ever happen.

Well, you've learned a little more about me.

Lexi Wright

6 | So-Called Life in 2018

This chapter explains my life in 2018. I have come up with a name for myself when I get big. I'm calling myself "*Internally Dead*". *America's Got Talent* was a huge letdown. I filled out all the paperwork needed to attend, printed the ticket they sent me, and practiced till my fingers literally bled. The day before, I get told we are not going. My dad saw the news and the line was already a mile long. I was very disappointed because I told everyone that I'd be there and on TV. I felt like a huge jerk. The next day, I didn't even touch my guitar. For a few months, I didn't touch it. After Christmas, I got back to it. Now, I have come up with a band name that I am calling myself. "*Internally Dead*". (I zone out sometimes and repeat things. I don't intend to do so). I have 9 albums sketched out. The first one, *Felicity*, (renamed to *Battle Scars*) consists of 13 songs and one instrumental. I have all the songs done for the second one, *Damaged Freedom*. I've passed out the CDs. Right now, I am creating the 7th CD, *Silent Disguise*. *Felicity* was released, January 21, 2018, and *Damaged Freedom* was released on May 27, 2018, *Dark Fury* was released August 4, 2018, *Cover This!* was released September 14, 2018, and *Shattered Skullz* was released October 12, 2018. Now I'm working on *Silent Disguise*. I already had *Felicity* completed

Starting Things Off Wright

before 2018 even hit. It was done in 2016. But I got so busy and forgot about it. I finally passed the CDs out in 2018. So really the release date is December 12, 2016. Not January of 2018. That's why *Damaged Freedom* was released in May of 2018. It was on its final stage of completion in the summer of 2017. So, at William's Graduation Party Concert I performed for him, I passed them out and signed them.

Lexi Wright

7 | My First Book

I began work on a nonfiction book called, *One Chance*, in late 2017. After the New Year, I finished it. I contacted a publisher and sent in my copy. They accepted it and asked for a payment of more than $700. Being poor, I cannot afford that much. So, I am waiting till I get some money to pay for it. After I pay them, I will have my book published and out there worldwide. And I will be getting that money back by being paid when someone buys my book. I will have a radio interview, and have a 30-second commercial on TV. So, I really want that, so I am waiting on money to pay for it all. Just recently, I found out the publishing company I contacted is a scam. So, I'm looking for different ones. I've found one that's linked with *Amazon* called, *CreateSpace*. I've looked them up and there are so many good reviews about them. It only costs $2.12 for printing costs. I get royalty payments, but not as much as I should get, but this isn't a source of income I'm relying on anyway. I'm getting my Social Security for Disability back here soon, so I will be okay with that. The book is just a side thing, just to say I have a book published. (Along with this one.) Not only have I written "*One Chance*", I have also begun work on 2 other books, AND finishing this one. The second book, *Chosen*, is a *Stephen King* style book and it is REALLY long

Starting Things Off Wright

and only containing one chapter. "*Fantasy*", my third and final book for now, is a narrative about how one girl meets the man of her dreams.

As of this very second, I have written my lyrics for *Silent Disguise*, got started work on the music, tried to create a website for myself, have close to 450 subscribers on *YouTube* and have a channel I work on every day besides Sunday, *Lexi WrightOFFICIAL*. I have music written for 1 out of 12 of my songs in *Silent Disguise*. I have finished *Shattered Skullz*. I performed at the annual talent show at my church. I played *Master of Puppets* in 2018 and I played my "Mary Jane" guitar. I didn't have "Starlight", my Jackson, yet. I was dressed exactly like James, and played and sang the song. My grandpa moved closer and lives in Beechmont now. Him and his girlfriend, Betsy, came to see me this year. Each time, Chris and his sister-in-law, Tina comes to see me. Mom, dad, William, and Dillon all go every year.

Lexi Wright

8 | Follow The Wright Path

William got accepted into *University of Cincinnati*, which was his second college choice. His first choice was *Ohio State*. I am really happy for him. I wanted to go to *CCM* and learn everything about Music. But I sadly don't have that opportunity. I am going to do everything I can to get out there. I will put my music onto a CD and try to sell a bunch of them or send it into record companies. I will try with every muscle in my body to get onto a talent show and win. I want this dream as bad as a baby wants milk. Every year, the Christian church in town has a talent show they call the Valentine's Day Banquet. They serve dinner and have different talents go up and perform in front of the whole church. In 2015, I did the talent show for the first time. Since I was into *Carrie Underwood*, I performed her song, "*Something in the Water*". The song was being played off *YouTube* from the backroom which the Youth Minister, Jimmy, was controlling. Well, during the song, *YouTube* buffered and Jimmy accidently cut me off. At first, I was totally bummed out and mad about it. I thought he did it on purpose. My mom was kind of upset about it, too. I ended up finding out what happened and he said it wasn't purposely cut off, the internet was slow. Which it is. The library's internet is way faster.

Starting Things Off Wright

The next year, 2016, I did the talent show again. I was still into *Carrie Underwood*, so I did her song, "*How Great Thou Art*". I was nervous to do this song because of the way the vocals are sang. I got this one recorded and it is on my *Facebook* page. I can't remember what I did for the 2017 talent show. I know I tried to do *Metallica*'s "*Creeping Death*" because of it being a bible story. I thought it'd be suitable for church. But Jimmy declined it. He said that he didn't think it'd be a good idea to do a rock song. I was like, 'okay.' So, I think I skipped it in 2017. But here in 2018, I was able to do a *Metallica* song. I asked Jimmy a week before if I could do a *Metallica* song, and he said, 'as long as it's clean.' I got pretty excited. I was like, '*Metallica*? Of course it's going to be clean.' So, the entire week, I practiced till I knew the words by heart. We called my grandpa and asked him if he'll come see me perform this year. He came up and filmed me off his phone. I was happy he came up. At first when I heard him say he was planning on coming, I shrugged it off. Usually when he says he's coming up, he ends up making an excuse not to. So, I was surprised he actually showed up.

2019's talent show, I'm hoping to do "*Master of Puppets*" again and dedicate my performance to my sister. I think that will be really cool. In my '*Felicity*" CD, there are at least 4 songs dedicated to her. I love her so much and wish every

Lexi Wright

day she could be here. And that's why when and IF I ever have children, I will name my first daughter after her. I have kept this a secret for so long and never told my mom. I want her to be proud that I named my first child after someone so special. To be completely honest, I am afraid to have sex. So, to have a daughter, I'd have to have sex. Two reasons that are really big. One: I'm just afraid to have sex, period. Two: I don't think I'll ever find anyone who would actually be attracted to me.

9 | Things Never Go as Planned

This year, since I was old enough, I did my own taxes. I'm not getting much back, only about $209. So, I made plans with my money. I want to make better videos on my channel, so I'm getting a better phone. I think my videos will be better if I had a good phone. And I'm getting my name legally changed to "Lexi Wright". I really want my name changed. I don't like my last name at all. Back when I was friends with no-name, in school, or just when I was 13, I got made fun of a lot because of my last name. So, ever since then, I wanted to change it. Once my grandpa told me about our relation to the Wright Bros., I thought that was a perfect last name. To put out my demos as a CD, I'm going to need CD's and cases. So, I'm going to go to *Microcenter* and get tons of CD's and cases. Only $1 for each CD and case! I figure once I put out my demo tape, I could make my first album, *Battle Scars*. And since I'm of age to do so, I'm buying myself a 20-sac of weed. I'm going to need a bowl and paper, so I'm buying that too. Plans always change. I never got to get the things I planned on getting, instead I got these *Metallica* figurines and a couple other things I can't remember what it is now. But I will get what I have planned out for my first SSI check.

Lexi Wright

My SSI check was supposed to be here soon, but I got a
letter in the mail today which said I've been denied again.
So, I'm setting up a court date to appeal against the
decision. I'm so thankful for all the *Wright Bros. and Wright
Sis.* I have. Every 50 subs, I make a special video. My goal
right now, is to reach 500. I'm at 443 right now, so only 57
away. I made 10 CD's total. I released "*Felicity*" in 2016,
"*Damaged Freedom*" 2018, "*Dark Fury*" in 2018, and "*Cover
This!*" in 2018. "*Lost Inside*" in 2018, "*Shattered Skullz*" in
2018. I am working on "*Silent Disguise*" now, which will be
released next year. "*Ace-Cide*" should be done in 2019, and
"*Walk with Rage*" also done in 2019. And "*Lightning Struck*"
in 2019. I hope to be discovered by the release of "*Walk with
Rage*". I am entering the Gourd Festival this year. I entered
last year and performed "*Master of Puppets*" in front of the
whole town! I didn't win, but I still had fun. This year, I am
doing "*Fuel*", since it is short and it is my favorite *Metallica*
song. So, I hope to perform it better than last year. I am
doing "*Felicity Idol*" again in February 2019. I am performing
a *Metallica* medley. I hope my performance for this is better
than last years, also. I hope to always keep improving. I
recently got interested in skateboarding. I can ride, but not
do any tricks yet. I am working on my ollie, but I am
missing the commitment. I finally got the ollies down,
about 3 months of practice. I went down this big hill in

Starting Things Off Wright

town and fell off my board and sprained my arm really bad. Though it hurts, I still ride and play my guitar. Anything you do could cause you pain in some way. But if you enjoy it, just do it.

Lexi Wright

10 | The Worst Mistake of My Life

Anger is one big thing I have trouble with. So, I know I need to get it under control. I'm working on getting into therapy and getting my SSI back. I have been diagnosed with bipolar disorder. So, I could be just fine, then all of a sudden get upset, angry, or even super depressed. I don't even know when or if that'll happen. I try to be calm, but I have trouble with it. So anyway, in September, I had an episode of bipolar anger and it got way out of control, even for me. When I'm angry, I try to get people to hurt me by either saying bad things to me or by actually hitting me. So, I was arguing with my mom about something that I cannot remember, and I was yelling from my room and I walk out to yell some more and mom is on the phone with the police. Now she was off work and dad was on his way back from work, and she was trying to get me into the hospital so I could get some mental/behavior help. Well, I saw her on the phone and I was calling her horrible names that I wish I could take back. Well, then I started saying bad things about my brother, Dillon. I was like, "He should just go to school instead of sitting on his ass just like dad! You know he's just like dad!" I didn't mean any of it, I was angry. Well, he got pretty mad and came out of his room and started punching me. I laid on the ground and just let him

Starting Things Off Wright

hit me. I was like, "Do it again! I like it!" He was super mad. Mom finally pulled him off me and he was walking back to his room, well now I was even madder, so I threw something at him and it missed him, but hit his hand. That made him madder, so he went into the kitchen, ripped the drawer out of the counter and pulled a butter knife out and threatened to use it on me. I put my skateboard in the way and it got a scratch. Mom grabbed Dillon and took him outside with her to wait for the cops. I followed and stole one of mom's cigarettes. The cops finally show up and mom and Dillon walked up and began talking to them. I was afraid they'd lie and I'd be in jail. So, I was like "They're lying!" The cop told me to shut up and I don't really like people telling me what to do, so I was like, "you know what?! F**k the police!" I showed them my middle finger then ran inside, and went out the back door and started to walk down the street. The neighbors across the way love to watch and see what happens to me, and they were all outside and one of them said, "out the back door!" I look and see them standing on their porch and no-name recording the whole thing. I just stopped and talked to the cop calmly. She didn't want to hear what I had to say at first, "I know I'll get jail time for this, but I smoke weed and I didn't have any, I smelled someone smoking, and so that pissed me off. I yelled at my mom and told Dillon to hit me.

Lexi Wright

He did and now all this happened." Well, she patted me
down and told me to sit in the back of the cop car, not
handcuffed. I was watching out the front window. Next
thing I know, they handcuff Dillon and my heart stopped.
They took him into the second cop car. As they pass me,
I'm screaming, "No! Don't take him! It's my entire fault!" I
saw the look on Dillon's face, he wanted to cry. I broke
down in tears. I've done juvi time, I didn't want him in that
life. Well, I get taken to the hospital, Dillon splits off and
heads to jail. I cried the whole way. Silently, because I knew
not to actually show any fear or weakness to the cops. We
get to the hospital and they check me in. I tell the nurses,
"What could I do to get me into jail?" They look at me like
I'm crazy, which I am. "Why do you want to go to jail?" One
asked me. I wanted to be in jail so that way I could have it
worse than Dillon. Adult jail is real jail, juvi is just a place
bad kids go for a while, not really any kind of jail, but they
still treat you bad. Well, I get into the behavior department
and have to talk to all these nurses. Then I'm waiting for
what seems like forever. By now, I've calmed down a lot,
and I felt like shit. Soon, one nurse comes in and tells me
they're releasing me. I call my mom for a ride home and I
get home and look at Dillon's bed. A tear rolled down my
face. I already missed him. Well mom and dad go to court
the next day and Dillon is released, but he can't be around

me for two weeks until his next court date. So, mom and dad got a hotel and used their free two weeks, they worked as housekeeper and maintenance, and Dillon stayed with them. Well, his court date finally comes and we all go. They call mom, dad, and Dillon into this little interview room. They talked for what seemed like forever. Finally, they come out. They dropped the charge from domestic violence to disorderly conduct. This is a BIG drop. We wait for a while, then they call me back. I tell them that I didn't want Dillon in trouble at all, I wanted him home. Remember, I TOLD Dillon to hit me, and ME and MOM were arguing, it wasn't even on him at all. I DRUG HIM INTO IT. Well, we wait some more, then Dillon gets taken back by himself and talks to the prosecutor or whatever. Then we go into the court room. I sit in one of the far back chairs. I see someone else walk in, and I just thought it was another PO or something. Nothing like what I'm about to say ever crossed my mind. I thought it was all over and Dillon was free again. But the judge was being a total ass. Dillon brought his computer to show that he was doing school online. The PO was like, "It's completed, but no dates." I rolled my eyes. Then they say mom never called the PO, which mom has the lady's number on her phone! Mom showed her the number, and the lady was like, "Yep, that's my number." So, what's the issue? Dillon stayed away from me as told, did

Lexi Wright

his school work, and mom called your sorry ass! Anyway, the judge says something about foster care and I spoke loudly, "I don't want that." The judge yelled at me. "That's my brother." I said once more. The judge continues and then threatens mom and dad to be in jail for Dillon's truancy issues. I felt tears roll down my face. The judge asked the lady that I saw walk in if she could take custody off Dillon. I couldn't hear or take much more. I burst out of the court room. William was waiting out in the waiting room because he wasn't part of it at all, I'm crying and I'm like, "They're taking Dillon to foster care!" I run outside and stand by the car and cry. Mom followed me out, she gives me a cigarette and she is crying too. We all were upset. Well, mom goes back in and finds out what's going on. Dillon is in juvi and will be taken to foster care the next day. When we get home, I smoke the ashes of weed left in our bowl, I get a little buzz, then I try to get a beer out of the fridge. I finally just cried myself to sleep. I couldn't believe Dillon was gone. It hurts so much because it's my fault. I need to get my anger under control. I hope Dillon is okay. I miss him already. And we don't get to see him again until sometime in November. I'm so mad at myself for making this happen.

Starting Things Off Wright

Good news, Dillon is out on probation for 3 years, he is not going to foster care. The only thing is, I spent the past two months away from home living with my grandpa. Mom and dad are doing everything they can to get me back home. I am not allowed to be around Dillon, because we have a stupid no contact order. So, now, December 8, I am back home for the weekend. I have to go BACK to live with my grandpa for at least 2 more days. Mom, dad, and Dillon all have court on Tuesday, and that is to decide whether or not I can come back home. I did learn one thing out of all this. EASE MY TEMPER. I've been working hard on that. I also lost ALOT of weight. I was 212, now I'm 194. I got my hair cut really short. Oh, and I have been working on my music. I've gotten *Shattered Skullz* done, I have lyrics written for *Silent Disguise, DisCOVER Me, Ace-Cide, Walk with Rage,* and *Lightning Struck.* I also have been making update videos on my *YouTube* channel; I currently have 472 subscribers, or *Wright Bros. and Sis.*

So, now, I am just waiting to see what happens within the last 22 days of this year. I can't believe I am going to be 20 years old next month.

Lexi Wright

11 | The Saddest Christmas Ever

Christmas. Usually, the time of year where I'd have the whole inside of the house decorated with lights, a small tree, paper decorations, and a wreath on the door. I'd play Christmas music from *YouTube*, and where I'd go to *Family Dollar* and buy less than $5 gifts for everyone, that way we get to open something.

But this year, none of that. The damn judge said we couldn't have Christmas together! I know, what a dick! You think I was depressed before? Try spending Christmas alone in a lonely apartment, with nothing to hardly eat, only faucet water to drink, and nobody there to talk to. This Christmas, was one of the worst. Crying myself to sleep almost every night because I want to go home.

Anyway, there are only 7 days left in this year. Let's see how this week goes. Merry Christmas to us.

12 | New Year's Wasn't Any Better

Today is New Year's Eve, December 31, 2018. And my grandpa's birthday. He is 63 this year, wow. Anyways, I just finished "*Lightning Struck*" and am moving on to "*War*". "*War*" is going to be all about fighting depression with everyday life, it seems like a war. So, yeah. I am going to have even MORE albums after that. So far in total, I have 16 CD's. And with me passing out 5 of each, well I think that's pretty good. The next CD, number 13, is going to be "*Total Destruction*", where life is a total destruction when you live with so many problems. CD number 14, "*Escape from Hell*", is about defeating depression and depression seems like you're living in hell, so escape from Hell. CD number 15, "*Defeat*" is the same thing, defeating depression. CD number 16, "*Freedom*" is the feeling of being free from everything I've had wrong with me.

Yeah, I'm making a lot of CDs. Let's just hope I get discovered soon. Happy New Year, goodbye 2018.

Well, next chapter will explain 2019 for me. What a year.

13 | So-Called Life in 2019

So, life is hanging on. The New Year's sucked. We didn't countdown or anything. Basically, screwed it up. Try again next year. I can't believe I am going to be 20 years old in

Lexi Wright

two weeks. Oh, I reached my *YouTube* goal! 511 subscribers! I am doing this 20-minute segmented episode thing called, "*Let's Make a Vlog*" and each segment is at least 5 minutes long. Segment one, "*Does That Really Work?*" is where I test products to see if they actually work or not. Segment two, "*Ranked!*" is where I take 5 bands/artists and rank them from 5 to 1. Segment three, "*Unlucky Satisfactory*", is where I choose a random note from a bag without looking and do what the note says. Segment 4, "*Fan's Chance*", is where everyone can ask me questions and I answer them, also where I'd open fan mail. It's been going good so far, made at least 4 episodes. My ultimate goal is to reach 1,000 subscribers. Let's hope for it! Oh, and I'm going to play "*One*" by *Metallica* on my guitar over at our church for the talent show next month. Can't wait!

14 | The Hell Within

I am still struggling hard with my depression. I am in therapy, which is going great actually. I see my therapist

Starting Things Off Wright

every Thursday at 3pm and we spend an hour talking and figuring out ways to help me win this war. Oh, that reminds me. I finished writing lyrics for "*Lightning Struck*", now I'm writing lyrics for "*War*". The title song I just wrote a few days ago. I think this one came out pretty good. Usually what I do is, write out the full album, make album art sketch, pre-record the lyrics, pre-record the music, then I sing with the music. I usually do about 4 songs like that a night for two nights, take a small break, then do it again until I get the whole album recorded. Then, I put the songs on my computer, modify them the best I can, then put in a blank CD, then make the CD. I haven't been able to make my CD's since "*Shattered Skullz*" though.

So, I do everything a whole band crew would do. I write my own lyrics, play the guitar, sing, record the music and vocals, compose the music, and distribute it.

William is going to college on my birthday. He is going to *Mount St. Joseph* somewhere in Delhi, Ohio. I am happy for him, but I regret my educational life. Now, I keep trying to tell Dillon, to follow William's path, not mine. He does a lot of the same things I do and I don't want him screwing up his life the way I did mine.

I'll be 20 tomorrow. Life is going by too fast. I'm young, but I feel old already. That's bad. Let's see how being 20 goes.

Lexi Wright

You know by now that *Metallica* is my all-time favorite band. Well, they are coming to Cincinnati and performing at *US Bank Arena* which is in Downtown Cincinnati. They are coming Wednesday, January 30, at 7:30pm. I am doing everything in my own power and ability to go. I really want to see them.

15 | Turn It Around

Being 20 doesn't feel different at all. I actually don't like it. I want to get younger instead.

Starting Things Off Wright

Well, William is officially a college freshman. I hope this pays off for him really well because he has done so much to get where he is now. I am hoping to get back in high school, get my diploma, go to college and major in music and minor in film. I really want to be a musician. So, I'm going to major my studies in music so I can learn as much as I can about music. Then I am going to minor my studies in film so I can learn all I can about filming and editing videos so I can hopefully grow and make my *YouTube* channel great. Which it is going pretty good so far. I am confused on one thing though, I keep hitting over 500 subscribers, but then I would see it at a later time back down below 500. I'm not sure what's going on.

16 | The Government Crash

Anyways, life is going great so far. I may not like what's going on right now, but we will somehow get through this.

Lexi Wright

Trust in God, have faith, and He will pull us through. I hope to see good things happening for us soon. The government actually shut down and it's going to make it real hard for us to get our taxes back. Which are supposed to be doubled. So instead of getting like $7,000, we will get like $14,000. Which will be great because we'll pay off our bills, and get a new place to live instead of Felicity.

I called my Social Security and asked about my claim. I'm supposed to get my SSI benefits back because it doesn't make any sense to me why I got kicked off of them because of turning 18. I should have legal rights to them. But whatever. So, I asked about my claim and they said it takes about a year to get an appeal court date. I filed for my benefits back in November of 2017. And they go back to when you filed for your first check, so by now, I should get at least $15,000 on my first check. After that, it's only going to be like $730 each month. Which is great for me.

Well, hopefully I get them soon. Let's see how the rest of this year goes. Oh, and this is the last year I'll write about. So, this chapter will be all about what's going on in 2019.

17 | Eggshells

It's really hard to live with my grandpa, because I feel like I'm walking on eggshells when he's around. He is so

Starting Things Off Wright

stressed out about things going on in his life, and with our situation. I think we all are. But he seems to snap at me for everything I do. Like for instance, if I don't feel hungry, and he makes dinner at 4-4:30 and tries to feed me, I say I'm not hungry then he gets mad, "Why don't you ever eat?!" I just cry a little inside and say "I don't know, I guess I'm not feeling good." Then he continues cooking, or he'll throw it away. It's like super hard to live over there as a smoker too. I'm working really hard on quitting, but that's a huge challenge for me. To not have a cigarette and have to deal with constant yelling or some sort of anger, now I know how mom and dad feel. I have to work on my anger and attitude. But that's going to be hard, too, because it's the type of person I am. I'm the type you'd see out there skateboarding, knocking over trash cans, graffiti up walls, attending high school/college parties, or just sitting around smoking weed and drinking all day. That's the type of person I am. I got tattoos and I play guitar, so I'm a rock n roll thug.

18 | Still Struggling

Lexi Wright

Life is so hard to hang on too. I meet up with my therapist every week and we talk about depression and harming myself. Not sure how that's supposed to help me, but okay. *Metallica* played at *US Bank Arena* in Cincinnati Wednesday, January 30, 2019, at 7:30PM, and they broke a record of the most people at *US Bank Arena*. Over 16,000 people were there! I was so upset we couldn't go. It would've been the best experience of my life! Cause I would've gone to a *Metallica* concert, seen James Hetfield in person, been the loudest one there, and hopefully, with the sign that I would've made, been let up on stage to play *Master of Puppets*! I was so sad that night. I was mostly worried for James' health, because I heard and saw a video that he fell in a hole on stage during another concert. The video said he had a concussion. So, I was pretty worried about him. Did I say anything yet? Can't remember if I did or not, but I love James Hetfield, I mean LOVE him. I truly believe that he is the sexiest person alive. He makes me smile, makes me laugh, and he makes me happy, all without even realizing it. That's magic. So, if I would've gone to that concert and seen him live and in person, I probably would have fainted. Or if I would've been actually let up on stage, I would've been ecstatic, star-struck, love-struck, oh, so many feelings would've over-powered me and I would've fainted, again. Probably why we didn't go.

Starting Things Off Wright

Anyway, my *YouTube* career has been going great. I still can't wait to reach 1K subscribers. Well, let's see how this month goes, and the rest of this year.

Lexi Wright

The church is supposed to have a talent show that they call the Valentine's Day Banquet. They have dinner, usually pasta, and the talent show. Most kids go up there to dance, beatbox, play DJ off their phone, or sing pop or rap songs. So, it was kind of weird for me to go up there last year and play a *Metallica* song. I really didn't like how that guitar sounded. When I was playing, I didn't realize how bad it sounded until I watched the video I made on *YouTube*. I was "in the zone". So, now I got a better guitar, I've been training my voice day after day, month after month, and been playing my guitar almost non-stop. So, I figured I'd go up there this year and play "*One*" and perform like never before. I was going to, too. But two weeks before, our youth minister, who helps out with the event, told me there was no talent show this year. He didn't tell me why, which was weird. But I figured it out through others I know. Instead of the talent show, they are playing the Newly-wed game for some reason. So, I'm not participating in that. Don't know why I would. Music. Music only. I was a little upset about it, but then I was like, "whatever".

20 | You Think You Get Me

Starting Things Off Wright

One thing that nobody gets about me is, actually two things. One, they don't understand why I am so weird about my phone. Ever since I got it activated and it had unlimited internet, I've been uploading *YouTube* videos almost non-stop. Gained more subscribers, more likes, more comments, I've been getting better things because of uploading constantly and staying so consistent. Well, my brother has to have my phone over the weekend while he stays down at my grandpa's in case there's an emergency. Out of all the days I've spent down there, there's never been one emergency. And I like to have my phone for a number of reasons, in case I actually do run into some fans, so I can post pictures on my *Instagram*, so I can vlog out here and things, so I can upload my videos at home instead of having to go to the library, and in case people call me, like my counselor or just anybody. So, I get upset if I can't have my phone and everyone is against me about it, like I'm crazy or insane. Everyone really does think and believe that I'm insane. I know it. Well now I only have 10 Gigs of data because my grandpa only bought a $45 card which gives me: unlimited talk and text, but only 10 Gigs of data, which sucks. Cause now, I can't upload any videos because the internet would be too slow and it'd run out within a week. I wish I could run my own stuff, have money to do so, and

Lexi Wright

just handle some things on my own rather than everyone doing everything for me. I'm 20, not 2.

Two, nobody understands my love for James. I feel like a stranger in my own home, in my family, because I'm different. I never liked older guys, just never did. I'm not real sure what it is about James, but he makes me feel so in love, it's literally crazy. What's weird is, I feel like I know him, connected, like I was married to him once before but something happened to me and here I am now. Which couldn't have happened. But I feel like we belong together. Every time I see his face, I smile. Each time I hear his voice, my ears perk up. Every time he laughs, I laugh. He gets hurt, I cry. He wins something or is very happy about something, I'm happy. So that's why if something terrible ever happens to him, I'd seek revenge and die with him. He dies, I die, too. We will always be together, even in death. Everyone says I'm insane, or crazy, or there's something wrong with me, because I love an older man so much. I don't know what it was, but when I saw his face for the first time November 3rd, 2016, I was in love. He looked like an angel, or something fell from Heaven. He was the sexiest person I ever saw. I was 17, and he was 53. But I didn't know how old he was yet. All I knew was his name and how sexy he was. In 2016, I felt what it felt like to fall in love for the first time. It was amazing. My eyes sparkled, my smile grew

Starting Things Off Wright

big, my heart skipped several beats, my breath escaped me, and I was very, very nervous. All through a picture of him! Think how it would be in person! OMG! Now, in 2019, I am still in love with him. Each day feels like the first, and it kills me to know that he will never feel the same way, and never, ever be mine. All my dreams, my thoughts, my life, is about him. I can't go one second without thinking about him. When I get depressed, sad, or angry, I don't want to think about James because in that moment, it makes me even sadder knowing how much I love him and how he will never love me back or ever be mine, ever. And that kills me. I am more in love with him than I was yesterday, and it still feels like the first time. I am so in love with James Hetfield, it is not even funny.

Lexi Wright

21 | Work, Work, Work

Ok, so I've been working with my parents at a *Michael's* store reset through *PeopleReady*. We are taking down the shelves, removing price tags, and throwing away the bad shelves and stocking up the good ones. We have this job for a week straight, and it's an 8-hour job. It pays well, so I'm keeping up with it so far. We have another job right after this one, pretty sure we're doing another store reset somewhere else. Again, pays well. We figured it up, after the next two weeks, I'll have close to $2,000. Just after these two jobs! I was like "Hell yeah!" I am going to buy my license and do the car auction with my parents one day. We actually got offered a really cool job today. We were the only ones working while everyone else just walked around, played on their phones, or just talked to each other. So, after work today, our supervisor told us he wanted to talk to us outside, away from everyone else. I thought we were in trouble for something. He told us he had a job offer where it's nation-wide, and for *dollar general* I'm pretty sure. In just one week, I'd make $1,100, and it's a month-long job for the whole year! So, every month I'd make $4,400, and every year $52,800. That's pretty good! And we'd be the bosses! So cool! One state he mentioned we could be working in was California. I can vlog it and make

Starting Things Off Wright

so many cool videos, boost my subscriber rate so much and get a lot of respect, or clout, on *YouTube* because of such videos all of a sudden being uploaded! I think that's so awesome! We are thinking about accepting the offer, after we move. We are moving out of Felicity. This town SUCKS! Burn it down, just kidding. No, but things do come your way, after a while. First, you go through lots and lots and lots of stress and hell, then, one day, you're blessed with something that could really help you out, or your dreams finally come true. I've been realizing that. I always thought that when I reached 20 years old, I'd be out on tours, rocking the world, have a record deal and tons of CD's out. But instead, I'm working my tail off for what I want. Not what I thought I'd be doing. Things will turn out great though, just keep praying, and trust in God.

Lexi Wright

22 | Stuck In Hell

Shit man, I don't even know what to say. I've been working and been buying things off *Metallica*'s website (www.metallica.com) and I'm a fifth member, so I got discounts on things I bought. I bought 4 magazines and that 'back to the front' book I've been wanting. I think I've spent $130 bucks in there at least! And I'm one to not care about myself at all. I care a lot about other people. So, only about 10% of my money that I've worked for only went to myself, 90% of it went to everyone else. I've bought lunch for everybody, bought my grandpa an *Apple* gift card, and bought mom and dad things. The way I am, it's everyone else before me. I'm last. Yeah, I might get a little upset sometimes because it's like, man, I wanted to buy something! But then, I'm like, well, others do come before me, and I like it that way. My faith is on a roller coaster, it's like I have hard times, then I have good times with it. I get really spiritual sometimes, other times, I'm struggling. But I always remember that God will help us through, even if I don't believe it at the time. And love, again, James first, me last. I think about James a lot. And he helps me through a lot of my hard times, even though he has no idea of my existence, more less my love for him so strong. I believe that I can't live without him, and I put him in second place

Starting Things Off Wright

in my life, of course after God, God is in first place, I dedicate a lot of what I do to James, and live my life as if I'm living to be James' right-hand girl, his cool, crazy, a little psycho girl. Always hungry for James. Yeah, I've texted him on his *Instagram*, told him I loved him, never got a response back, but I can tell it's been read. So, he knows I love him, but he doesn't know that I *love* him so truly. I'm also a romantic person. When it comes to love, I get pretty romantic. I look mean all the time, but I'm the nicest person you'll ever come across. The reason I look mean and ready to fight, is because I'm holding so much pain and sorrow deep under my skin and no-one will ever know. I want to smile and be happy, but it feels unnatural to smile, and so normal to frown and just let myself be whatever. Like I said, I don't care about myself at all. Everyone comes before me. And some people think that's crazy. This book is almost finished. Just a few more things, hoping to add my dream come true, either becoming the rockstar I want to be, or by getting the love of my life, James Alan Hetfield. He will always hold a special place in my heart. I'm his other half, his best thing that'll ever happen to him, his best joy in life, his everything, and he'll never, ever realize that. This stabs me right in the heart. Anyways, I'm going to go take a nap because I'm falling asleep writing this. Let's see how the rest of 2019 goes. Hopefully good.

Lexi Wright

It's May 29th, yes, I haven't been writing for a while. Been so busy. We moved, but stayed in Felicity. We moved into a crappier trailer and William and Dillon have the biggest attitudes ever since we moved in, which was like, what, 10 days ago or so? One thing they are mad about is, we have to get Kiki and Roxy on the okay, or get rid of them, because our landlord said they are restricted breeds. Another thing they are mad about is, the place we live in. The walls ain't finished, no carpet down, the doors ain't built right, the old, crappy, type of windows you have to open with a handle, and how it feels like a sauna. Dad keeps trying to tell them, we got a roof over our heads, and we ain't living in a box on the streets. I'm not trying to put it all on them, I got my issues too. I got my medication finally, been on it since May 15th. I was trying to keep Ktulu inside for a while, because I was afraid it would be the same incident like our first cat, Tiger. Tiger used to get out and go hunt, then he'd come back. When we moved to Felicity, he got scared and meowed all night. Dad got tired of his meowing and thought he'd come back after a while, he never did. But, instead of understanding me, they don't listen, like usual. Ktulu escapes and I worry about him. The landlord said he was trying to make the trailer park a nice place, get rid of all the drug-addicts, and clean it up a bit. Well, there have

Starting Things Off Wright

already been a few things happening. A stabbing over a lost dog, drug trafficking in some of the trailers, random gunshots, yeah, I don't think it's getting nicer. I've been staying with my parents instead of going to pawpaw's like I'm supposed to. We got the okay for me to attend family therapy every Tuesday at 5:30-7:30. August 1st, is our next court date, which we're all hoping will be the one where the judge lets me back home. I'll let you know. I got close to 700 subscribers on my *YouTube* three times. Can't wait till I actually pass it. My vertigo is acting up right now. I still love James. It feels like the first time, every time. I want to be a metalhead, so I'm expanding my playlist, discovering more bands, I like the type of music with lots of screaming, fast playing, hardcore metal. I'm making a battle jacket like James Hetfield's. I've been working on my music a lot. Trying to come up with a cool name. I came up with, *Internally Dead, Ktulu, Unholy Desolation, The Primordial,* and *Screams of Sins.* I kept *Ktulu* for a while, but I'm going back to *Internally Dead* and keeping it there. I made a few recordings of me playing my guitar and been trying to make my own music, all on my own. It's not easy. (A song of mine ☺) I still suffer with Depression and it seems to be a bigger roller coaster since I got on my medication. Hopefully I can get it straightened out. I've made over 100 cover videos on my channel. Some good reviews, most bad. But I'm going to

Lexi Wright

keep trying. Never give up. You CAN achieve your dreams. And I know one day, I will. *Internally Dead* will be rocking the world soon. Back to James, I'm a little upset he changed his looks. He's still sexy, though. But it seems like after I told him how I truly feel about him, he goes and shaves off his goatee, grows out his mustache, and let his hair get longer. He doesn't look the same, but it makes me realize, it's not about what someone looks like that makes them sexy, although he was VERY sexy, it's who they are. And James is the most amazing person on the planet. After every show, they donate $75,000 to a food bank in the town they played in. James and I have so much in common. I'm a lot like him. I honestly believe I am his other half, his one and only, the one who should've been there instead of his wife. He needs to be mine, because we'd both be SO MUCH happier. James Hetfield is the love of my life. I love you, James. I didn't know you could crave weed. My mouth gets dry, I drool, and sometimes I get shaky. Anyways, I hope to go home for good in August, achieve my dreams soon, and for James to realize how my love for him is real and true. Oh, one more thing. We only eat once a day now, I've lost some weight. So, we're scrounging right now. Always happens that way. Anyway, going home because mom gets off work in 5 minutes, she works at *Lowe's* in Beechmont, Ohio.

23 | Stolen Freedom

I'm at the library right now checking my *YouTube* analytics, and writing this. Some kid just said he's going to get a fire started. Should I be worried? Nah. Anyway, dad has super paranoia. He thinks Dillon's P.O. knows I'm home, recognizes me, and knows my every whereabouts. I'd hate to be so paranoid like that. Yes, I got anxiety, but I guess I just don't care what happens to me. If something happened to anyone else, I'd be sad. I have no care or respect for myself, at all. All my care and respect goes to everyone else. I hate thinking about myself; I feel that it's EVERYONE else before me, in absolutely anything. Now that we're hardly eating anymore, I really make sure everyone gets to the food before I do, and if there's anything left, and then I go after it. We're like wild wolves every time food comes in the house. Last time I got weighed, I was 186 lbs. This means I lost about 24 pounds! I kind of want to be anorexic, I want the skinny part, but everything else stops me, plus, I can't control myself when I'm hungry, depends on HOW hungry I am. I've been cleaning the house for the past week, going through the boxes, untangling wires, throwing trash away, and putting things where they need to go. There was SO much trash when I first got started, a week ago. Not even ¼ of a way in

Lexi Wright

yet. Yesterday, I got ¾ of it done, again, SO much trash. Today, I was going to finish it, but mom wanted to do it so she knew where everything was going. She threw out a lot of trash, too. I always write about James each time I add something else. (I just realized this is going to be a LONG chapter, and a LONG book) I've been wearing my bullet belt. I want to get my hair cut to look like James', get tattoos, and try to look like him the best of my ability. Anyway, about James now. I know he is 56, going to be 57 this year. He is 36 years older than me, and I DON'T CARE. I love him and that's all that matters. I believe that once you get above 18 years of age, then age does not matter when it comes to love. Yes, I realize that James is old enough to be my grandfather, but I have NO care in the world about that, like I said, I love him. I guess what I'm about to say is either psychosis or some form of schizophrenia, lol. But I kept lying to everyone saying that James comes over at 2 am, takes me on dates, and I call and text him on my phone and *Facebook*. Well, I sometimes think he IS coming over at 2 am and I stay up until then just to figure out it was part of my lie. I've also been "texting" him; I try to make it look so real; they have to believe me. I do that on *Facebook*, too. Now I believe that I AM dating James Hetfield. Congratulations Lexi in 2017, you made 2019 Lexi seem insane. In exactly a half hour, we

Starting Things Off Wright

have to meet the family therapist. I hate it. Oh, I came up with the lead and rhythm guitar parts for my song, "No Sleep till Then". I have to get music made because I actually got my first real gig at *Lawrenceburg Event Center* in Indiana on August 3rd. And on November 15th, I'm doing *America's Got Talent* in Louisville Kentucky. I need at least 2 songs, which I chose already. *Whiplash* and *For Whom the Bell Tolls*. I've gotten pretty good at playing guitar. Tapping is my specialty. No one seems to agree with my style of music, hardcore metal, which I intend to play. *Internally Dead* is going to be a hardcore metal, one-person band. Doesn't sound possible, does it? Well, it is. Everyone will see that I can perform a four-person sounding song, all by myself, because I can't find anybody to jam with, so I have to do it on my own. Which stresses me out A LOT. Anyway, right now, I have 701 subs on *YouTube*, love James endlessly, and in need of a cigarette and guitar playing. So, I'm going to go rehearse for both shows for 2 months, then 3 months after that, starting now. It is June 4, 2019. Let's rock this world!!!!!!!!!

Lexi Wright
Some pics of my life so far:

I got my first *Metallica* CD, "*Ride the Lightning*."

Family Dinner at *Cracker Barrel*, Christmas

I played the same guitar James Hetfield played.

(His Signature Series Vulture)

I was at Blue Ash Park and the sun was in my eyes

24 | The Love of My Life

I got two songs written out of seven. I got a setlist made and I'm going to play covers and originals. I'm hoping to make it as a rockstar. Which I realized is VERY stressful and gives you anxiety sometimes. I live my life as if I AM a rockstar, just living life and enjoying some time off or something. 703 subs now. I still struggle with depression, I want it to die away from me, but it's sadly not possible. One thing weird about me is, I get lost in music, don't matter what I'm listening to, I get lost in the music. Like right now, I'm listening to *WEBN*, or *102.7 THE LUNATIC FRINGE!* And *Ozzy Osbourne's "Mama, I'm Coming Home"* is playing. I can't stop thinking about James! Seems like he's the only thing I think about anymore. Ok, here. Here's a picture from when I FIRST laid eyes on him, which was love at first sight:

Lexi Wright

That was in 2016, I first heard *"Wherever I May Roam"* from Dillon's DVD player in his room, and first heard *Metallica*. I was helping him clean up. I was like, "Play that Egyptian song again." I thought the intro sounded like something from Egypt for some reason. He played it again. I liked the song. I was like, "Who is this?" Wow. He was like, "Um...*Metallica*." I had NO IDEA who they were or what. I mean, I've heard some songs being played from dad from his computer, but I never paid attention, I was into country at the time. But then I asked, "What's the singer's name?" and Dillon grabbed his CD case and pulled out the booklet, it had their pictures on there, there were also some lyrics. He named them off and I just kept asking who the singer was. He's like, "James Hetfield." Nobody knew, not even me, that I'd end up loving the guy so much. I went to my room and looked up James Hetfield in 2016, and came up with pictures like the one above. I seriously couldn't take my eyes off him, my jaw even dropped to the floor! I was love struck! ☺ Then years went on, and now, he's all I think about.

Starting Things Off Wright

Here's him in 2017:

I still thought he was sexy. Here's him in 2018:

I STILL loved him. Him in 2019:

Lexi Wright

I was saddened when I saw him like this. It seems as if he let himself go. But I STILL love him. I worry about him a lot. He just doesn't know, or seem to understand how much I truly love him and how my love for him his real. I honestly don't care about money, at all. I grew up poor; money holds no value to me. I think it's stupid how money works. I think it's just paper with a face and number on it and we trade it for something we want, it's just some kind of trade system. I don't even like having money because, really, what am I going to use it for? Someone else might actually need it. If I buy anything, it's either, cigarettes or something with *Metallica*'s name on it. Yes, I like to collect anything with *Metallica*'s name on it, but like I said, someone else could use it for more useful things, like food or clothes. I don't know maybe I'm just weird or something. Check this out, here's a quote by me:

Starting Things Off Wright

So, it's like, love is better than money. Oh, and I totally despise gold-diggers. They piss me of so much. Rich people make me mad, too. They believe money is their god, like are you insane or what's happening here? When the stock market crashed in 1929, rich people jumped out windows, shot themselves, hung themselves, just went berserk, because their "god" let them down, was gone, no more. And the poor people were just fine, because they already had nothing. So, it was like seeing the world go insane while you just sit there watching for entertainment. This caused the Great Depression. But anyway, you see what I'm getting at, right? I don't love James for his money, I love him for him. I think he is a good person, so kind, laid-back, and a total badass. I love his tattoos; I think he looks like a bad boy, if you would, or an outlaw, a cool kid, a person who doesn't give a fuck. And we share A LOT in common. I've learned a lot about him and somethings I found out, I was like, "Wow, we seriously do have a good number of things in common."

Lexi Wright

Oh, before I forget, here's my collection of *Metallica* so far:

There are a few things that are not in the picture because I got them after this photo was taken.

Some things are: My *Metallica* hat, a few shirts, the Back to the Front book, a *Kill 'em All* cassette, and for some reason only Lars and Kirk are seen. I think they should make a Cliff Burton figurine, since they did everyone else like the *Master of Puppets* era, aka 1986.

25 | This Hell Surrounds Me

Depression still seems to take over my body and mind. I don't feel alive when depressed, I feel like I'm actually dead, because I am numb, no care, no feelings left, and no tears are able to fall from my eyes anymore. I want to rid this feeling from me but I don't know how. No one wants to be around me when I'm trapped in the dark shadows of hell. I understand. William and Dillon don't have depression, so they don't know what it's like. I'm jealous, because I wish to be happy, and here they can turn anger into something funny. Another thing, I feel like God is betraying me lately. He's been there for William numerous times, giving him money like crazy, and William said, "It's not my responsibility to feed you." Which is right, but he could help out with food instead of leaving us to starve and buying shit for him and Dillon. God's been there for dad, mom, and everyone else. He's just like, leaving me to drown in the deep waters of sadness and betrayal. I suffocate in the fog of hate my brothers have towards me. Like I said, they've had big attitudes since we've moved, but they REALLY have it in for me. If I say something, anything, they ignore me and turn away. Someone mentions my name, they cringe. And for some reason, Kiki's bark makes my ears ring and it hurts, probably because I listen to a lot of

Lexi Wright

my music up so loud. But I try and tell them, nicely, that Kiki's bark hurts my ears, and they DON'T CARE. They make her bark, get mad when I say something. Oh, and this morning, William was getting in the fridge to eat breakfast, well, Roxy was almost completely in the fridge, William, did NOTHING. See, in our family, well, me, mom, and dad, don't let the dogs near our food, unless it's on the floor or we directly give it to them. They are NOT allowed to be ANYWHERE around our food. AND, they get disciplined when they do something wrong, like shit and piss on the floor, or run out the door. They usually get rewarded when they do good. When we discipline them, we don't beat them, we spank them, tell them 'bad dog!' and 'go lay down!'. If they did something terrible, like when Kiki killed a kitten, or Shadow bites another dog, they get swatted and put in the cage. But William and Dillon baby them. The dogs can get away with murder. William or Dillon eats, like say, dinner, the dogs sit right next to them, put their nose on the plate, and nearly take their food, oh, and that's okay. The dogs run away, we get animal control called on us, the boys get them back, the dogs go in their room, and everything's fine. They don't care about the Animal Control call, or that we have to pay a fine of $250, and go to court! But, if I discipline the dogs, tell Kiki to shut up, or get out of the fridge, anything, I'm being mean to them, I'm

Starting Things Off Wright

hateful, I'm *abusing* them. Well, really, I can't blame the dogs for being confused. They get babied by 2/5 of us, disciplined by 3/5 of us. So, they really don't know the difference between right and wrong. That makes me sad. I love those dogs, they are family, but I just want them to be *good dogs*.

Shadow used to be my dog, I went to *Genesis Behavior School*, I was 10, it was 2009, when I came home from school one day, mom and dad waited for me to get off the bus, they were like, "We have a surprise for you. It's upstairs." I'm pretty sure I've been asking for another cat since Tiger's disappearance, so I thought they got me a cat. I rushed upstairs to our apartment, and saw a little black puppy. Mom and dad said, "We just got her. She's your dog." I can't remember why they got me a dog, but they did. They let me choose the name, I think. I picked *Shadow*. We used to always go by the color of their fur to determine their name. So Shadow was supposed to be my dog since 2009, it's 2019. So, it's like, I discipline her for doing wrong, and praise her for being good. She still seems to understand the difference between right and wrong. She gets scared when I throw fits or yell, but other than that she loves her family.

Lexi Wright

We got Kiki because Pawpaw got William a dog from one of his friends. He was a German Shepherd mix. His name was Rudy. The neighbors lied and said Rudy was a youngster and not sick or anything. Well, when we got Rudy home, to the trailer, he just laid in the hall, not moving. We just thought, he's being a lazy dog, we didn't realize what was to come. We woke up one morning, and Rudy was in the hall again. We tried to take him outside, but he didn't move, not even his tail. Dad got him to get up and outside. Rudy went underneath our porch and William tried to get him out, Rudy growled at him and Dad said, "Leave him alone." Rudy ended up going to puppy heaven. Turned out, he was somewhere between 10 and 15 years old. So, we wrapped him in an old rug, took him to *East Fork* and dropped him off. We didn't know what else to do with a dog like that. William was pretty upset, so a few years later, me and mom went to *Payless Mini Mart* one night, and there was a guy giving away puppies. Mom stopped and asked what kind they were. "Pit-bull and Rottweiler." They guy said. Mom said no, and went home. I raced mom inside, and told dad about the puppies. He said "what kind?" and I told him. Mom comes in now, and dad said, "Go get one." See, mom was surprised because dad never wanted a pit-bull because he didn't trust them. Me and mom rushed back over to *Payless* and got a puppy. I'm pretty sure this is 2012. Dad

Starting Things Off Wright

said this dog is William's because of Rudy. Then, a year or two later, Kiki gets out and gets with another dog. That following year, she gave birth to a litter of puppies. We kept one, but gave away the rest. So, Roxy ended up becoming Dillon's dog. So now all three of us had a dog. I have always been a huge cat-person. Me and dad were walking up to *Payless* one day while mom was at work. I heard meowing and saw a tiny kitten. I picked it up and asked the guy if I could have the cat. He said sure. I was happy because I had a kitten. It's 2018. I took the cat into my room and set him on my bed gently. I was petting him and letting him know he was okay. After a while, I started listening to some music. I turned on a *Metallica* song and his ears perked up. He walked over to me and climbed into my lap, laid down and purred. I was like, "No way. My cat likes *Metallica*!" So, I named him after *Metallica*, his name became Ktulu, which is a mythical creature that lurks beneath the sea, that *Metallica* made up. So, I had a cat and Shadow became mom and dad's dog. Now, everyone had a pet and was happy, I thought. The pets ain't just our individual pets, they are the family pets, too.

Lexi Wright

26 | Small-Town Skater

Anyway, I'm working on my ollies and have improved, a lot. I used to get off the ground about an inch or so, now it's like a foot. I'm excited because I've been practicing for almost a year.

Now it's:

1. Fakie Ollie
2. Boneless
3. Shuv-It
4. Pop Shuv-It
5. Frontside Pop Shuv-It
6. Frontside 180
7. Backside 180
8. Half-Cab

Then I'll be pretty good after I learn these. I can Ollie, but not moving, yet. I'm working on that before I move one to another trick. After I learn these beginner tricks, I'll learn these:

1. Kickflip
2. Heelflip
3. Frontside Boardslide
4. Backside Boardslide
5. Frontside 50-50
6. Backside 50-50
7. Manual
8. Nose Manual
9. Frontside 5-0
10.   Backside 5-0
11. Nollie
12.   Switch Ollie

Those are intermediate tricks. Here are the advanced/pro tricks I'll learn after the intermediate ones:

1. Nollie Flips
2. Switch Flips
3. 180 Flips
4. 360 Flip
5. Tre-Flip
6. Smith Grinds
7. Feeble Grinds

Lexi Wright

8. Lip-slides

9. Nose Grinds and Crooked Grinds

I won't learn these until probably 2025, lol. No, but I can't wait to be a good skater. I love skateboarding, it's fun and I get to do something cool. I always wanted to invent my own tricks that look cool, but I gave up that. I'll still be a good skater. I don't want to make anything out of myself from skating, just a rockstar is all I want to be.

27 | The Worst Criminal

So, I feel like I'm a most wanted criminal or something. I have to hide from the law, I'm on the run, can't do anything or I'll get in trouble. Right now, I'm hiding at the library from CPS, if they see me AT ALL, everyone's life is over. We all go to jail. My mom had to go to the hospital last night because she had chest pain, felt like passing out, and felt like throwing up. I called her 'ask a nurse' number on her medical card, explained what was going on, and they said to hang up and dial 911. I got a sick feeling in my stomach. I dialed 911 and explained to them what happened, they sent out an ambulance. The paramedics that came, they were having a bad day or something, because they were acting like mom was just faking it or something. They took forever inside the ambulance, which scared me. Turns out, they were hooking mom up to a cardiovascular monitor, trying to get an I.V., and get vitals. Then, one paramedic comes out and talks to dad, he's like, "She looks really exhausted, is she always like that?" You could tell he had an attitude. My dad kept cool and told him mom got a new job and that we just moved in. The paramedic said, "Ok, I was wondering." And got in and drove off to the hospital. Me and dad followed. Dad thought it'd be faster to go down 52 because there are no stoplights. Dad looked in his rearview

Lexi Wright

mirror at one point, "I think that's them behind us." I didn't think they went down 52 to get to the hospital, usually they take 125, since we were going to *Anderson Hospital*. We stopped at *Speedway* and got gas, when we turned in the driveway, dad looked and noticed it was the same ambulance. So apparently, they took 222 towards Chilo and took the long route for some reason. We got gas then got back on the road. We got to the hospital and they were coming out with the stretcher, which means they just dropped her off. We go in and see her, and she has to get blood drawn, do a few tests, and rest for a few. Every three hours, they'd do another cardiovascular test. Everything came back okay. Finally, about 2 in the morning, they give her prescriptions, and tell her all was wrong is she had a UTI Infection. That didn't sound right to me, but you know, whatever. I'm trying SUPER hard to hold in a fart, because I know it's going to be a good one and I don't want to let it loose. I was so tired I wasn't thinking straight. We got home about 3:45 in the morning. I got up about 12 noon today. I've been working on a skateboard movie, so I filmed the intro scene. Go across the living room, show me playing guitar, and I got a phone call about our band. I'm trying to make it about a small-town skateboarder, roams the streets, surfing the road and coming home to rock out. A skateboarder who is in an upcoming rock band and

Starting Things Off Wright

working hard to make it work. Also, the rockstar
skateboarder finds love towards the end of the movie. A
kick-ass, hard rock, skateboarding romance movie. Ever
since I've learned that James skated in his teenage years, I
took it on. Before that, I never wanted to touch a
skateboard, I was so afraid of it. When I saw that James was
skating the streets, going about 60 mph, I had to have no
fear and skate. I learned the basic basics. Ride. Just ride.
Now, I'm learning tricks. I'm learning the *Shuv-It* now. I can
do an Ollie, Fakie Ollie, and a Boneless. Three tricks in.
Right now, I have NO IDEA how to do a *Shuv-It*, so I'm
trying to learn it. I almost twisted my ankle yesterday,
because I tried to be tough and take the Skater Trainers off
and try to do an Ollie like normal. I did two just fine, went
to do another, and wiped out. My pinky toe and the left
foot hurts a little, but I just got a bruise and a little scratch.

Lexi Wright

27 | Help Wanted

Anyways, about James now. Dad keeps making fun of him, which makes me very sad. I know I'm in the wrong for liking an older man so much. Turns out, it's called *Reverse Pedophilia*.

English

Noun

reverse pedophile (*plural* reverse pedophiles)

(slang) A young person who is attracted to older people and has repeated sexual thoughts or urges.

Synonyms

reverse pedo (informal)

See also

teleiophile

So, I could be a registered sex offender technically. Which is bad. I mean, I love James; I'm not wanting to hurt him at all. I joke around and say that I'll rape him, but that's because I know he's married for one, and for two, he wouldn't want to have sexual actions with me, because I'm young and he is older, and he'd possibly get in trouble with the law. I'm the one trying to sexually act upon him, and

Starting Things Off Wright

he's the victim in this case, and he'd still be the one to get arrested. I mean I wouldn't actually *do it*, it's just a joke. If I saw James in front of me, I'd probably just freeze and go completely numb, or I'd have a deadly heart attack because the one I love so much is right in front of me.

Lexi Wright

28 | No Home, No Job

Let's face it; the way my life went, we'd knew this would happen, right? So, you know the entire situation and what went down last year, but I haven't written in what feels like such a long time. We had court August 1st, which was to talk about me coming home. Well, I ruined that. Mom, dad, and even Dillon, was telling me to stay inside. Hold up, I was staying with pawpaw and he moved out in May, thus giving me nowhere else to turn but Mom and Dad. They did NOT want to take me in because they knew they were risking jail time. But they let me stay, so though we lied to everyone saying I still lived with Pawpaw, I was staying in the house the whole time. Everyone told me to stay inside because they knew we'd get caught if the probation officer saw me wandering about Felicity. I didn't believe them, I thought they were being too paranoid about the situation. I mean probation was out watching via surveillance like the fucking FBI! That's one thing that makes me mad, like why you got get so FBI on us? And no one seems to understand me on that. Anyway, so when mom and dad came back from court, they told me to pack my bags. I thought they were joking, as you can tell, I don't care about the situation, I just care about what happens to everyone else besides me. They were not joking. What happened in court was, the probation was angry. "Don't try and lie, I already know." Kristen said as she called Mom, Dad, and Dillon into the confrontation room. Mom and Dad exchanged worried glances. Mom sighed and told her the whole story. Then Kristen turns to Dillon, "They are making you sick with all this lying ain't they?" Dillon had a cold and was obviously not feeling too hot. "No." He said. Kristen gave him the evil eye. "You feel better now that it's in the open right?" Dillon was confused. "No." How in the world could lying give him a cold? Just asking. They get into court and the judge was in a good mood. Kristen follows them in. The judge reads Kristen's e-mail, and was furious. "YOU WANT TO GO TO JAIL TODAY?!" Mom, Dad, and Dillon all sunk into themselves. "Uh, no sir." Dad said. I didn't get every detail on what happened, but that's the gist of it. I got taken down to *James Saul's Homeless Shelter* at 5pm that day. I did not like it. I ended up getting used to it after about a week. I walked up to McDonald's EVERYDAY for Wi-Fi, kept up with my YouTube, applied for jobs, and looked for housing. For the first 4 days, I would NOT eat at the shelter. I was afraid to eat after anyone because I heard someone had Hepatitis. I wanted no part of that, so I began losing weight. When I entered the Shelter, I was 212, after that week, I was 191, a week later, 184.7. I was dropping pounds like butter. On August 7th, this girl named Jazalyn moves in. We

Lexi Wright

became friends instantly. We hang out for a week straight before she wakes me up at 2 in the morning saying she got paid. We've been trying to get out to her mom's house for some weed. I haven't smoked in a year, and I was totally down for it. We called for a Lyft and filled out all the paperwork needed to leave. We get out to Winton Terrace in Downtown Cincinnati and get inside a little after 3 am. Jazalyn went and talked to her mom, who was furious about her bringing me and her boyfriend along. Jazalyn told me and Austen, her boyfriend, to start cleaning. That was the deal, clean the house, you get to smoke weed. I did the dishes while Austen swept the floor and mopped. We got the house live-able clean at around 6 in the morning. I was whooped. Jazalyn goes and tells her mom that we cleaned the house so well you can live in it again. Her mom was happy about that. Jazalyn told me her mom wanted to meet me, so I walk in with her. After about awhile of talking we finally start smoking. I took the first hit and it hit me like a freight-train. My eyes grew wide, and I was short of breath. "Wow." I said, handing the joint to Jazalyn. We passed that joint around till it was gone. This brought us up to about 8 in the morning. We found an old mattress, threw my blanket down on it as a sheet and just laid down and went to sleep. I'll tell you what, going to bed blazed is not a good idea. I had nightmares that night, so scary I got panic attacks, and panicking while high is not a good idea either, I got paranoid high and started freaking out so bad I woke Jazalyn up. I kept thinking the cops were outside, and I kept hearing someone knocking on the door. I finally calmed down and got some sleep about 12 noon. When we woke up, it was going on 5 o'clock at night. I called my mom and she didn't answer until around 9 o'clock. By then, I was already stoned again. Turns out, she sent the cops out to look for me. I wasn't lost, I didn't run away, I left. There's a difference.

While I was at the shelter, I learned how to take 5-minute showers, eat really fast, and just do my chore without being asked. Staying with Jazalyn might not be a good idea, she has three kids and is not that great of a parent. I mean, she doesn't beat them or neglect them, but she constantly yells at them and allows them to cuss. Not my place to judge or anything, but I just don't want to be a part of that kind of parenting. Jazalyn wants me to be her friend and the kids' aunt. I have no clue on how to deal with kids. Especially if they were to do something wrong under my watch.

Well, mom and dad finally got through to me by calling back. I answered and they were worried sick. "Where are you?!" Mom asked. I told her where I was and why I left the shelter. I didn't include the weed, because I was afraid she'd

Lexi Wright

be mad at me for leaving the shelter just to get high. Which is what I did. Don't ever follow my path. Anyway, Jazalyn's mom wanted to talk to my mom, so I handed her the phone. "Is she incompetent?" She was asking my mom if I was slow, or mentally damaged, which I believe I sort of am. At first, mom was actually going to let me stay for a couple days, but dad told her that the neighborhood I was in wasn't a good one for white people. So, they ended up coming up to get me. I re-packed my stuff, slowly and confusingly, because I was boiled. I went out for a cigarette and they come pulling up. I go back in to get my stuff and Jazalyn and Austen help me. I put my stuff in the trunk and just got in the back seat because I wanted to hide me being stoned as much as I could. I asked mom for a cigarette and smoked that, which increased my high. Jazalyn was talking to mom about what happened and about getting a trailer out in Felicity. Austen was talking to dad, and dad didn't want to talk, he wanted to leave. After a while, Jazalyn and Austen went back inside and we left. It felt weird for me to be in the back seat, going home, stoned. I almost fell asleep, or overdosed, a few times on the way back. We stopped at Taco Bell for dinner and just got it to go and ate it at the house. When I walked in, I went straight to tell Dillon that I was stoned. He could tell. I had a roach, half a joint, in my pocket, so the next day, I got stoned again. After the roach

Starting Things Off Wright

was gone, that was it. Ever since, I've been staying with mom and dad again, but this time I'm staying indoors. But mom, dad, and Dillon are all scared someone is going to see me and they'll go to jail. So, they are going to take me back to *James Saul's Homeless Shelter* sometime this week. I left that place for two reasons, one, I didn't trust nobody, and two, to get high. It just didn't seem safe there to me, but I'm usually wrong about everything, so maybe it was the safest place I could be.

Lexi Wright

29 | Tattoos and Changes

You know how I am about James Hetfield by now. I ordered fake tattoo sleeves, got my hair cut and died it blonde, put a temporary tattoo on my neck, and modified a fake mustache into a fake goatee. I dress in black anyway, so now with all that, I kind of look like James did back in 2013. After about a week or so, the tattoo on my neck faded off, good thing I snapped some photos. Anyway, today is September 13, 2019, and the Gourd Festival is tonight at 7:30. I really wanted to go but with the situation still going on, I can't. If I go, I'm risking jail time for everyone, including me. Which I don't care about me, I just care about everyone else. So being stuck inside, I figured I'd do the lip-sync here, still having fun, I guess. So, yeah, the situation has changed me a lot. I have more of an attitude and I'm getting skinnier because I refuse to eat. How am I surviving? I just drink a lot of liquids and eat small meals every now and then. Last night, my stomach was in so much pain, I almost had mom and dad take me to *Anderson Hospital.* I took some medicine, and fell asleep, so we didn't go. This morning when I woke up, my stomach hurt still and I threw up 3 times. I fell back to sleep and when I woke up this time, I felt better. So as of right this very second, I looked at my subscriber count and I have 1,321 subscribers!

Starting Things Off Wright

My next ultimate goal is 5k. It took me 4 years to get 1k, but I'm already 300 in to 1k, so it is moving quick, but it should move somewhat faster. I want to reach 5k before 4 years, which would be 2023. Hopefully by then, I have like 10k or so.

Anyways, on the next page is an illustration I drew of me and I autographed it. If you would like me to sign this book, I will sign it under my current autograph or somewhere, you can choose. If you would like to meet me one day, I'll have meet and greets from both my YouTube career and Darkness Prevails concerts. I can't wait to add a paragraph or so on my first concert. You know that I've been changing my band name like crazy, but trust me, I'm sticking with Darkness Prevails forever. So, here's my illustration and autograph.

Lexi Wright

30 | The 2016 Darkness Prevails Interview

Anyways, I thought of a cool chapter I could add. The interview I did myself back in 2016 and uploaded to my YouTube channel. I'll make another chapter called, 'Life after Success', if I hopefully win *America's Got Talent*.

Please tell us, when you were born? Thursday, January 14, 1999 at 11:57PM

What's your full name and are you proud of it? *Madison Marie Sack, and no. I changed it to Lexi Marie Wright because I got made fun of a lot for my last name. Some names they called me were pretty bad and vulgar.*

Are you named after someone, if yes then after whom? *My middle name is from my mom. We don't really name anyone after anybody.*

Where are you from and are you proud of it? *Cincinnati, Ohio, and not really. I don't really like this state too much. But who does? (Laugh)*

Do you love playing any sports, or just watching it? *I like to play basketball and skateboard. I despise watching golf on TV, but I can play it, which is kind of weird, I guess.*

Lexi Wright

Which one is better, Basketball or Baseball? *I like both, but if I had to choose, I'd go with Basketball*

Who is your favorite person in modern history? *No one. Unless we're talking 21st century, then it'd have to be James Hetfield from Metallica.*

Who is your favorite writer in modern history? *Don't have one. I used to read those Dork Diaries and Diary of a Wimpy Kid books.*

Who is your favorite musician from 20th century? *Metallica. No one seems to like anything they put out after the Black Album, but I like almost every song they've released. I think that Metallica can't have a bad song, like it's impossible or something.*

Which one you prefer, *Daft punk* or *Gorillaz*? *Neither, never heard of them.*

Do you love animals, if yes then which one you love most? *Yes, I love cats a lot. Funny thing is, I'm also scared of them because they eat you when you die, same with dogs. If I had a choice, I'd definitely choose a cat over a dog.*

Do you have children? And how many? *No. I don't want any because I'm scared, I wouldn't be able to handle it. I don't want to ruin their life because of me not knowing what I'm doing.*

Starting Things Off Wright

Then again, it'd be cool to be able to tell someone else what to do. (Laugh)

How many children do you want to have, if you did have any? *I want to have a daughter named Amberlee. Now I would be naming her after someone else, my sister. I wish she could be here today, but you know, things happen.*

Are you married or single, and why? *Single, because I'm saving myself for the real one. Hopefully James. (Laugh)*

If you are not married, when are you going to get married? *I don't really want to live the married life. Yes, being single also sucks, but it has its moments, you know?*

What is your favorite drink of all? *Dr. Pepper. Want to know my toe size, too? (Laugh)*

Do you have favorite basketball player? *No. I don't really get into sports too much. I like the Cincinnati Bengals, but I don't get too hyped when they do something or whatever.*

What is your greatest achievement in high school? *I was starting to get good grades and turn my life around, but then it all got ruined after some bullying, which caused me to drop-out in 10th grade.*

Lexi Wright

Are you proud of your points in high school? *No. If I could restart my whole life, I'd do a hell of a lot better.*

Do you want to have a business? *Yes. I want to succeed in YouTube.*

Which business you want to have and why? *A YouTube career, because then I could help out my family a lot.*

What is your most favorite scene from movies? *Any James Hetfield scenes, or fights, or street racing. I mostly like comedies, though.*

If you love snakes, which one is your favorite? *I don't like snakes too much, but if I had to choose, I'd go with the anaconda. My dad is terrified of snakes, btw.*

Do you love music? Which genre is your favorite? *Yes, rock and metal*

Please tell me, which one is your favorite: old school rap or today's new age rappers? *I don't dig rap too much. I like Eminem and N.W.A., that's it.*

How tall are you? Have you dreamed being ever taller? *About 5' 7", no. Just something else people would make fun of me for. "How's the weather up there?" (Laugh)*

Starting Things Off Wright

What is your favorite number and please tell us, why? *7, because it is my lucky number and a holy number.*

Have you ever been on any bridge? Do you like bridges? *I've crossed the Kentucky bridge into Ohio, the bridge into Indiana, no I do not like bridges.*

Do you have fear of anything? If it's not secret, please tell us what you fear the most? *SLUGS!!!!!!!!*

Where are you working right now? *At home, I'm a YouTuber. I've also started writing a book. Could I add this interview in it? It's an autobiography, I'm wanting to add all the cool things.*

Sure. Have you ever dreamed of being successful lawyer? *Um….no not really. (Laugh)*

Which actor is your favorite, Al Pacino or Robert De Niro? *Neither, if I had to choose, then I guess Adam Sandler.*

Where do you want to travel? *Colorado is my dream destination because of the legal pot. (Laugh)*

Which ocean is your favorite and why? *I am terrified of oceans because it's just open water. Like, miles and miles of water. If I ever got lost in the ocean somehow, I'd be so scared, I'd have a heart attack probably.*

Lexi Wright

Have you ever been in Europe? Where? *Not yet. Hopefully soon with Darkness Prevails.*

Do you love history? Did you have high grades in history classes? *I hated history*

Do you believe that Trump will make America great again? *Yes. I think he'll be the best president we ever had. People don't like him because he tells it how it is and puts God back in America.*

Have you the right to vote in US elections? *Yes, I do.*

Which candidate was your favorite during latest US Presidential elections? *I didn't like any of them. Obama was the worst though.*

How do you describe yourself? *Laid-back, loving, selfless, and a badass. (Laugh)*

Can you describe yourself in just 3 words? *A bad-ass (Laugh)*

What are the most powerful 3 words that changed your life? *Hoping, "Yes, yes, yes, yes!" from America's Got Talent in a few months.*

Who you admire the most, mother or father? *Mother, but I love them both.*

Do you have siblings? How many? *3, two brothers, and a sister*

Starting Things Off Wright

How many books do you read during summer vacations? *1. Not really a reader. Did you know I started reading when I was 3? I was able to read chapter books. My parents were able to recite the Cat-in-the-hat book because I had them read that to me every night before bed.*

How many books you have read in 2015? *Not sure*

Are you a technology lover, if not, why? *kind of*

What do you prefer, *Windows* or *Mac*? *Windows*

Which brand is your favorite, *Apple* or *Samsung*? *I hate Apple.*

Which Operational system's user are you, IOs or Android? *Android*

Who is your favorite male *Youtuber*? *Faze Rug*

Who is your favorite female *YouTuber*? *NerdForge*

How do you feel right now? *Tired and a little achy*

Can you remember the first time you felt angry? *Not really, I've been angry a lot*

Can you remember the first time you laughed? *no*

Who is your favorite comedy movies actor? *Adam Sandler*

Lexi Wright

Who are your favorite stand-up Comedians and why? *Kevin Hart, because he's just hilarious.*

Which *Home Alone* movie is your favorite? *The first one*

When was the last time you cried? *Last night. Then again, I'm always crying on the inside where nobody can see the tears fall.*

That's very sad. What was the reason you cried the last time? *I felt imprisoned into my home*

Do you know where will be your career in 10 years? *Hopefully a major successful rockstar*

Do you love your work and is this your dream work? *I love my YouTube work, but it's my second choice if being a rockstar doesn't work out, if it does, then I could still be a YouTuber, just not as much*

What is your favorite moment from childhood? *Hanging out with my brothers*

Which is your favorite animal and why? *Cats, they mind their business and have no care for what they do*

Do you have pets, Cat or dog? *I have three dogs and one cat. Kiki, Roxy, Shadow, and Ktulu*

Starting Things Off Wright

Do you love fishing, if yes then why? *I don't love it, but I like it, it's relaxing*

Which is your favorite Burger and why? *The chicken sandwich from McDonald's, with extra mayonnaise*

Which one you prefer, *Coke* or *Pepsi*? *Coke*

Hopefully you learned a bit about me. ☺

Lexi Wright

31 | Superstisous

Now I'm not quite sure what's going on with this family. Every one of us have secrets and we're all sneaking around behind each other's back. For mom, I think it's sad to say that she is a gold-digger and she doesn't want to admit it. Don't quote me on this chapter, because I could be highly wrong on this. Anyway, I also think that she is seeing another guy. I'm scared to death to tell dad about my suspicion on that, because it would cause an argument and possibly a divorce, and I don't want that. The reason I think she is seeing another guy is because like say, she says she's going to the store and we know how long it takes to get there and back, and she's gone for a couple hours sometimes. Today she has community service she has to do because she got caught stealing $400 out of the cash register at *Lowe's*. She was immediately terminated, or fired. I don't want to say these things about my mother, but it's my suspicions, and I'm free to speak my mind, so I'm including everything that happens in my life into this book.

Now for dad, man, he cheated on mom a couple years ago with some chick he met on Facebook. He was going to *East Fork Lake State Park* with her almost every day. "I need a break; I'm going to *East Fork* for a little bit." He'd take the truck and be gone for hours. That ended in an argument and big fight which led to mom getting arrested because she was hitting all of us and screaming at us. Mom told me to unplug the landline we had, and dad would tell me not to, I didn't know who to listen to, I unplugged it. "Oh, you're on mom's side." No, I wasn't on anybody's side, I just unplugged it so mom couldn't call the police or dad couldn't answer it if that lady was brave enough to call him. Mom actually got her number and called her and told her off. I can't remember what exactly she said, but she let that lady know dad was moms. The suspicion I have on dad is he doesn't know how to deal with us because of the way his childhood went. He thinks we are stupid and don't know how to do things. Yesterday, we painted the house, which was actually Dillon's punishment because he got suspended from school because he yelled at the teacher for help on his work and was saying vulgar things with other kids in class. So, dad made him paint the living room and kitchen. At first, dad taped up the ceiling in one spot and starting edging that area in, then painted that area. After he painted that wall, he quit. "I'm having trouble doing it. You guys do it." Dillon painted one whole wall and asked me to hide in mom and dad's room because he wanted to open the window for fresh air while he painted the next wall. I wanted to help him, not only to help, but also because I enjoyed painting. I played "Rummy 500" with mom and dad while Dillon finished painting.

I'm going to try and not make my chapters only one page long, but this one might be only one page. Sometimes that happens, I guess. Remember, don't quote me on these because like I said, I could be insanely wrong.

32 | The Scary Things I've Seen

*This chapter may scare the young and faint of heart, so discretion is advised.

This is all true. Let's start all the way back to when I was 9 years old. The house we lived in was pretty haunted. Me and Dillon were playing in the living room, now we are on top off the garage here, which is about 6-10 feet in the air, and we saw someone walk past the window. It didn't look right, like a person. It was long and very skinny. Had to be about 10 feet tall to walk past the window. It didn't scare us, it confused us because we knew something wasn't right about the thing. We asked each other, "did you see that?" and both of us in fact did see the same exact thing.

Another time when I was 9. For some reason, I always wanted to build a clubhouse. In the backyard, there was this bush that we used to hide in and play around and everything else. I got the idea to turn it into a clubhouse so I asked Dillon if he wanted to help me with it. At this time, he was only 6. This part I hate to include. We were sitting by the back door which was in the basement going over the rules and figuring out a name for the 'club'. I asked Dillon to come up with a phone number and he gave out 6 numbers. I said "we need one more number to that, because that's only 6 numbers." Out of the blue, he got pissed. "YOU BITCH! GO TO HELL!" He didn't look right when he yelled at me, he looked pretty scary actually. His eyes were all white and glossy and he looked taller than he actually was. There was a growl to his voice when he yelled at me. I got scared and ran and told dad what happened. Dillon never heard those words before and for him to say that shit, there's something not right. Later that night, we were playing in the basement again. We saw a shadow figure dart past us and go into the laundry room. Dillon thought it was a vampire and got an eraser and stuck nails in it and sat it on my bed. "When the vampire goes to sleep, he'll get poked by these nails and run away." I went upstairs for something I can't remember, but when I came back downstairs, I forgot about the eraser-nails thing he made and laid on my bed. I jumped up and Dillon pulled it out of my back. After that, we started to lay down for bedtime. William was already asleep. Me and Dillon were having trouble sleeping, and started to talk about the clubhouse again. Well, the room started to get hot, very hot. I saw a flash of fire in a circle on the floor, it formed the evil shape I hate and will not describe any further, well, it formed that shape and flames came out of it and went back down. When the flames disappeared, the devil stood there, growling, snarling, looking at me and Dillon. I was terrified. I screamed for mom and he just vanished, no fire, no smoke, just gone. Dillon was so scared he was bawling his eyes out; I was crying too. He says to this day, he saw what looked like cartoon ghosts when he was crying. That was very, very terrifying.

This was when I was 10. We've moved to Felicity and gotten an apartment. I was, again, going to bed when this happened. We had a cat named Tiger, whom I miss so much. Well, he was sitting on the counter and was staring at me, wide eyes and a scared look in his eye. I'm thinking he yawned, but what I saw was fire coming out of his mouth and red eyes. "There's fire coming out of Tiger's mouth!" I screamed. Something was definitely wrong. Another time when I was 10. I will never forget this nightmare. Me, William, and Dillon were talking in the kitchen. There were dishes in the drain board. William and Dillon had their backs to the counter and I was standing in front of them talking about, again, a clubhouse I wanted to make called "KSE" or "Kids for Saving Earth" I saw on the internet. Well, I noticed one of the cups lift up into the air and drop. I got scared in my dream and scared myself awake.

Lexi Wright

This was when I was 13. We've moved to a trailer in Felicity. Me and Dillon were in the living room talking about school. I was homeschooled and Dillon was going to regular school. We both noticed something white in the kitchen. Dillon asked me, "what did you see?" I said, "a white middle finger." Dillon's jaw dropped. We both saw it. Again, when I was 13, I was in my room watching TV when it kept shutting off on its own. Dillon tested the TV and it shut off. I turned off the light and Dillon came out to tell me the TV was broken. I saw someone sitting on top of the TV and asked Dillon if he saw it, he said no. I know there was someone there because you could she a dress, legs, arms resting across the legs, and a scary face glaring at me smiling.

I was 14 here. I was in my room watching movies off my tablet when I noticed movement on my wall. There were two shadow figures there. One had a gun and the other didn't. The one with the gun pointed it at the other one and shot him, he fell to his knees, then face down. Then they disappeared. I saw that almost every night. There was no sound of the gun for a while, but then you could hear the gunshot and see blood splatter out the guys back. All silhouetted.

I didn't see anything else until I was 18. I was recording a YouTube video in my room when I noticed someone

Starting Things Off Wright

watching me from outside my door. There was a hole in my door and it was just standing there watching me. I was scared, but I told it to leave. It would, then it'd come back. It kept playing with me. I stuffed clothes into the hole just so I wouldn't see it. This was when I was 18 also. I printed out a picture of Metallica and turned it into a poster. I hung it up on my wall and I shouldn't have done that, because you can feel the band members watching you, even if you're not looking at it or anything. One time, James on the poster, smiled. I got scared and took down the poster. After a while, I hung it back up.

This was when I was 20. I was staying with my grandpa and there was something very, very creepy there. There have been multiple times I have seen this thing. The first time I saw it, it was a mist and it was by the door of the apartment. It scared me, ever since that happened, I'd see things in the corner of my eye, always in the kitchen or the living room. I used to sleep on the couch in the living room, but once I started seeing that, I never went into the living room alone. This is the last thing I've seen so far.

Lexi Wright

33 | It's The Roarin'-20's Again

So, it is nearing the end of 2019 and I can't even begin to believe it's about to be 2020. It just doesn't seem real. The end of the world has been a speculation and interest to some since 2012. Everyone keeps waiting, studying, or even guessing when the end times are going to happen. Fact is, it already is happening. We are living the end times now. It doesn't seem like it because it's not what we thought, what we began to speculate about the end times. I believe I know how the world is going to end, when and why. But this is not about that, this book is about my life and how I lived. Aside from the end of the world, the apocalypse and everything else, my YouTube career is something I want to talk about. I started YouTube back in June of 2015, first video was me trying to get on *Good Mythical Morning* for their little ending video they do before the *Wheel of Mythicality*. After that video, I began to learn about posting videos, vlogging, and being consistent on my uploads. I didn't know about monetization or getting paid for uploading videos until 2017. I thought I could upload videos of whatever and get paid for it. I learned that was not the option, you cannot upload anything that is copyrighted. I am not getting paid yet. But I will be. On October 10th, I will begin a

whole new side of my YouTube channel. I used to upload
videos like, me drawing something, cover songs, music
videos, lyric videos, stuff like that. But now, it's going to
change for the better. My videos will be me being me.
Pranks, stupidity, random shit, just originality from the
heart of the darkness that I've prevailed. I'm stuck at
1,280 subscribers at this moment. It seems to jump back
and forth between 1,270 and 1,280. It is October 6, 2019,
and we have court on the 10th. I'm hoping to be able to
step outside again without worries. Because it would
benefit us all for good. I've been sick with the flu for the
past week and have not been wanting to do anything but
sleep. On the 1st, I learned that James Hetfield went into
rehab for alcohol addiction. He did the same back in
2005 and seemed to be sober for years. When I heard the
news, I was devastated. I worry about him because of his
age, and lately he hasn't been looking to happy or healthy
in his pictures. He's all I think about and all I ever want
in life. I cried my heart out when I read the post *Metallica*
put up on *Facebook*. The main thing I worry about is that
something bad happens to him while in rehab. People are
nuts there. I don't want him in there, but what can I do? I
can pray and pray that he'll be okay, but lately my faith
has been drowned out. I've been having so much trouble

Lexi Wright

with my faith I almost don't believe anymore. I want to cry right now.

A little something I want James Hetfield to know: James, you are the only one I love so truly. I care so much about you and want the best for you. You in rehab makes me so sad and angry at myself because I feel guilty for telling you how I feel about you on your Instagram. I really wish I could take it back. I'm sorry I made you feel bad. I know it's my fault for what happened since 2018. Ever since you let your hair grow out and began drinking again, I know it's my fault and I'm sorry.

If you haven't already known, I told James I loved him on *Instagram* back in 2018. I built up the courage and typed the message. It took me a minute to send it, but I did. Three days later, I notice it's been read. I began sending him three romantic messages every three days. Something like, "your name is my favorite word", or something to that effect. I'd tell him I loved him every day, hoping to land a spot in his life. He is the only person I want in my life; I no longer want to be a part of this family; I want to go my own way and be the musician I was meant to be. I want to leave but I can't. I'm lost, trying to figure things out on my own, no help from anyone. I thought I had it figured out when I left the homeless shelter with my 'friend'. But mom and dad came and picked me up. Got screwed on that plan. I was going to get a job and get an apartment and everything, but no. I had to get picked up from my parents. Not going to lie, I was scared being on my own like that, but that's part of life. I'd like to make a confession. I'm afraid of my dad and that's why I want to leave. When he gets mad, he hits us, seems like me the most. I get mad when he hits me and I enjoy being hit, so I try harder to make him mad just to get hit. I love the pain, the feeling I get from the pain feels good to me, makes me sad instead of angry, lets out *my* pain...

Sorry, I'm crying now. I realize that now I'm afraid of men, all men. I began to think that all men are the same. So, how can I love James if I'm afraid of him? You tell me...

So, court got rescheduled until November 7th, don't know why. I signed up for *America's Got Talent* again. They are coming to Louisville KY. The audition ain't until the 19th, but I've been practicing. I talked it over with my parents and let them know that this is not for me, but for everyone else. Mainly for James, though he has no idea what I do and go through for him. Back in 2015, I did the talent show in town and was very nervous. I'm trying to figure out that if I can't sing in front of 900 people in a small town, then how am I going to sing in front of 4,000? Exactly. But I keep telling myself that there is no time for failure, no option to back out. It's something I have to do. I want to thank James for inspiring me. I love

Lexi Wright

80's rock music, especially with synth. I'm going to do "*Foolin'*" by *Def Leppard*. I only have 90 seconds to change my life forever. I modified the song to be only 90 seconds long. I have to practice two songs in case the judges ask for a second song. Hoping they won't. "*Of Wolf and Man*" by *Metallica* is my second song choice. The audition ain't all there is to it, there's *Judge Cuts, Live Shows,* or *Quarter Finals, Semi-Finals,* and *the finale.* I'll start out in Louisville, then travel to Los Angeles for the *Judge Cuts.* If I win that, I travel to Hollywood to put on a live show. Everything else is there. It's going to be a hard battle for me, but I have to do it. Today is November 06. I got two weeks to make sure I got these songs packed down tight. No messing up, no turning back. If I win the finale, then I get $1,000,000 and headline Vegas. I put a hold on my YouTube career to see if my dreams of becoming a rockstar finally happens. So, I won't be able to write for a while, but if I get chances to be on my computer, then I'll add little updates. This is my only chance to achieve my dreams, to change my life, to become what I'm meant to be. Ok, I have to go rehearse now, lol, going to have to get used to it. Hey, it's what I dreamed of, let's make it happen, make it real. James, I love you.

34 | SHIT

Fucked over again! I didn't audition because I had no ride out to Louisville. I can't believe how many times I get screwed over. Its Christmas time in 2019 and I am very sad because all I wanted was to be a rockstar and I can't. Fucking sucks. Sad to say but the whole rockstar dream is dead. Darkness Prevails no longer exists unless someone else actually makes it real. I gave it all up, deleted my YouTube channel because I ain't getting anywhere with it. I wanted to make my parents happy and proud. With the money, I was going to surprise each of my family members with one thing they always wanted but could never afford AND give them a split of my money. Everyone was going to be happy, or so I thought. It took me four years to reach over 1,000 subscribers. But that's over now. Let me explain what happened. I watched *The Dirt* from *Motley Crue* and really got into it like, "I'm going to be a rockstar just like they are!" I saw the whole "sex, drugs, and rock n' roll" cliché. Not what I wanted out of it. After the movie, I began thinking hard about it. I got the idea of wanting to be famous and help my family financially back in 2012 when I was 13. I wanted to be a magician or an actress at first. That went straight to the toilet 3 years later in 2015. Magic faded from my interests and I thought of becoming a country

Lexi Wright

artist instead. I wanted to follow Carrie Underwood's path. I came up with a nice sounding name to go by, too. "Lexi Wright". That idea only lasted for a year when I discovered rock n' roll. It was late fall of 2016, November 3, 2016. William and Dillon were asked to clean their room. Earlier that year, I bought Dillon a *Metallica* CD with no idea on who they were. I got him the *Black Album*. Well, he was playing it in his DVD player while he cleaned his room. I wandered in there and began helping him clean his room. *Wherever I May Roam* came on and I asked Dillon what song it was. Long story short, I ended up falling in love with James that November. I wanted to have James as my own, so I got started on guitar and trained my voice to match his. I thought of many different names to call my act. I thought I was going to make it big. So, I found out, it's not going to happen, so I gave it up.

So, what's the use of this book then? I can still have a cool story to tell, I guess. So, I guess this is my life now, battling depression and killing every demon in sight. It is December 16, 2019 right now. It is 3:15 in the morning. I need sleep, so goodbye for now and I will see you on the next page of my life later on. Oh, and I didn't give up James, he is still the one I love. Never give up on love, but it makes me very sad though. I began thinking, "how can you love someone who will never love you back?" sorry, I'm crying now. I love him so much and just wish he could understand the pain of how much I love and care about him. Love fucking hurts, bro! Fuck love! James is the only person I will ever love and I will never forget him. I feel like a total ass for falling in love. I feel like he hates me, or it's my fault he's in rehab. Anyway, see ya on the next page of life. Not chapter, yet, next page.

Guess the song..." Die! Die! Die! Die! Die by my hand, I creep across the land, die by my hand, killing first born man!" *Creeping Death* by *Metallica*. ☺

So let me explain how Christmas went this year. We each got $25 from Pawpaw and $40 from mom and dad. At first, Dillon made his Christmas list for his counselor so I thought it was just him getting Christmas this year, just the same as last year, I was pretty mad. I got so mad I ended up going to the psych at the hospital. Got released the same night and the nurses there lied and said mom and dad were still mad at me and didn't want to talk to me on the phone for a ride home, so instead they called a taxi to take me downtown to some homeless shelter for men only. The staff gave me directions from *Google Maps* to the women's shelter. I began following the directions, ended up on Columbia Parkway exit on the highway, so I turned around and went back to the shelter. At first the staff wouldn't let me in, I sat down and thought I was done for. Someone

Lexi Wright

finally opens the door and asked what I wanted. "Can I use the phone to call my parents really quick?" The lady let me call mom and dad. I told them where I was and within 45 minutes, they came and got me. I was in yet another part of town that was not good for white people, my fucking luck, right? I get home and couldn't sleep so I was up all night that night. Sucked.

Today, we went to *Eastgate Mall* and walked around looking for something to get for Christmas. I was looking for *Metallica* stuff and stoner things. Ended up walking out of the mall with a pair of nun-chucks. Dad has a bunch of knives, name off a few, the machete, kukri, parang, a dagger that goes between your fingers, a buck knife, and a pocket knife. Dillon has a dagger. I'm not allowed to have a knife because they're afraid I'll kill myself with it. I want a Glock 47 just in case I ever get brave enough to end it all, but mom won't allow guns or motorcycles in the family. Anyways, we picked William up from his friend's house and when we came home, I noticed the internet was out, which got me super depressed. I got on moms' phone and ordered a Camaro to build. I'm going to paint it to look so fucking cool, give it lights, just make it a total badass car that flashes to the beat of *Ride the Lightning* by *Metallica*. It's going to take up to 2 weeks or so before it arrives. I'll include a before and after picture below on the next page.

Starting Things Off Wright

Oh, and I'm not sure if I said anything yet or not, but Darkness Prevails is over. I gave it up because it wasn't going anywhere. I've been working very hard on my career since 2015. Since nothing is happening with it, I made a quitting video and posted it. Never made a video since. I even gave up guitar and singing. I quit because it's not worth fighting for if it's never going to happen. I truly believe that *America's Got Talent* is my ticket to fame and stardom. I'm starting to think that if I would've gone, I would've won all the way through, got famous through the years, not been able to handle it or something, and either died of suicide or drug overdose. Or I would've been able to meet James since I was famous and would've had a massive heart attack or something. Probably the whole entire reason we never go.

James has been making me sad lately. ***We've been texting on *Facebook* and been going out every Friday night for the past 2 years. Well, I got the feeling that he felt I was just into him for his money. I tried to prove to him that wasn't true at all. I got some beer and drank while I texted him on Wednesday earlier this week. Out of the entire conversation, he wanted to take a break from this relationship for a minute. I begged him not to, but he didn't respond. I got so sad. On Friday, I told him I was going to be at *Eastgate Mall* today and asked if he wanted to meet

Lexi Wright

me there. He said he'd think about it, but I ended up seeing him there, which was great. He bought us all some *Wendy's* for dinner, which was nice. After dinner, me and James talked for a minute, then we kissed and he left. A nice Saturday it was.*** So, on the next page you will find the before and after photos of my super badass Camaro. I need a cigarette and some video games need played, not really a gamer, but I'm bored because the internet is out right now, so yeah. Merry Christmas!

Starting Things Off Wright

From top to bottom: Front End, Left Side, Back, Inside Details, Further Away, Right Angle

I really wanted to make everyone's life better with the money I would've gotten from *YouTube*, but as you know, it didn't work out. So, maybe I can still achieve one of my dreams of making my family happy from the money I get from boxing. MAYBE. I got a free class on Monday to try out and see if I even like it, then if I do like it, then the membership is really up there in price, but I could possibly

Lexi Wright

continue to go with the membership to become a real boxer. I think that'd be pretty cool. KICK SOME ASS!!

I wanted to be a badass rockstar so fucking bad, but hey, boxing might be cool too.

Fuck man, James is the fucking best. I love him so much. I like guns, Camaros, motorcycles, basically anything that makes me a badass motherfucker.

Well, it's about to be New Year's, 2020, can't believe it. So, I just hope 2020 is better. For my birthday, we're either going to go roller-skating, get a tattoo, or get drunk since I'm turning 21. I want to get high on weed instead, but beggars can't be choosers is what I heard. Sometimes love is the most amazing thing ever, other times it hurts like hell. Seems like that's the way it's going for me and James. Sometimes he makes me feel so in love, like magic is real, makes me smile just thinking of him, makes my heart beat faster, can't sleep at night because I'm constantly thinking of him, can't hardly eat because thinking of him makes me feel like throwing up and nervous, I still force the food down my throat because I got to eat. Other times, he makes me sad because he doesn't take the time to read my messages and realize my love for him is so true and real, makes me worried because of his age and being in rehab. One thing I learned from loving James so much is that it's not about how someone looks makes them attractive, although he's sexy as hell, it's about who they are. And James is a great person, so nice, loving, kind, and self-less. I want to make one thing clear, very clear; I don't love James because he's got money to buy the world, I love him for him. HONEST SPEECH.

Well, let's see how 2020 goes.

Alrighty, its 2020! New Year's, again, sucked. I watched the ball drop while sort of high on weed candy. I had a doctor's appointment today for my chest, because for about a month it's been hurting me and making it hard to sleep. Every time I lay down, it tightens up and makes me short of breath, but then I lean forward and it relieves it. First, I went to urgent care in Amelia, they refused to see me and told me I was having a heart attack. "I'm pretty sure I would know if I was having a heart attack." I spoke. They told me to go to the ER. Instead, the next day, we went to a different urgent care. Again, they told me to go to the hospital. I got upset because it seemed like no-one was listening to me. We finally go to the ER and they couldn't find a problem with me. I was upset. Today, at the doctor's office in New Richmond, they told me it was depression-based pain. I got mad because it didn't seem right. The whole ride home

Lexi Wright

sucked for mom. Well, my birthday is coming up. Not really excited about it.

I'm in the wrong for this, I know, but I'm very afraid of everyone in this family. I wish I could go somewhere, but I can't. I'm afraid of disappointing dad because he likes to be right and have the last word, and sometimes hit us. I'm afraid of Dillon because he's the one who gave me vertigo. Dad hits hard, but he knows how to stop himself, Dillon don't. I also think they don't like me. I'm afraid of William because he thinks he's smarter than everyone and likes to put you down. I don't know if I'm misreading, crazy, or what, but it REALLY seems like neither of them like me at all. I'm afraid of mom because, she's the only mother I got and I don't want to disappoint her.

Not sure if I said something yet or not, but I realized something else about my love for James. I see him as a father-figure. Sad, I know. My dad has always been there physically, but not mentally or emotionally.

I'm trying to figure out what's meant for my life. Since the day I turned 13, I wanted to have a life worth living. First thing I EVER wanted to be was a veterinarian. That lasted for only a second because then magic moved in, and you know the rest. I'm thinking I might be cursed or something. Only bad things happen in my life, never anything good.

Starting Things Off Wright

I'm trying to learn how to be emotionless because I think that would benefit everyone. Never getting mad, sad, or depressed. Just a plain face unable to feel. (Yeah, I thought I'd be good at writing songs, too.) I'll be 21 in less than 2 weeks; I'll write about it afterwards. Oh, yeah, I forgot 2019 was the last year I was going to write about, well it is. I'll include my 21st birthday, then that's it. See you after my birthday.

Lexi Wright

35 | Something Random

Everyone has favorites. Here, you'll learn about mine.

1. Movie – *Karate Kid (2010)*
2. Animated TV Show – *Family Guy*
3. TV Show – *Roseanne*
4. Song of all time – *Fuel* by *Metallica*
5. Band –*Metallica*
6. Car – Camaro
7. Animal – Cat
8. Color – Midnight Blue
9. Sport – Skateboarding
10. Game – *GTA: San Andreas*
11. Drink – Mountain Dew: Voltage
12. Alcoholic Drink – *Bud light*
13. Thing to do – Sleep
14. Book – *So Let It Be Written*
15. Place – A cabin in the woods
16. Restaurant – Skyline
17. Smell – Weed
18. Person in the whole world – James Hetfield
19. Season – Summer
20. Month – August
21. Weapon of choice – Glock 47

Starting Things Off Wright

22.   Chat site – *Facebook*
23.   Time of night – 12 am
24.   Youtuber – *Faze Rug*
25.   Age to be – 12
26.   Day of the week – Friday
27.   Destination – Colorado
28.   Holiday – Christmas
29.   Summer Activity – Swimming
30.   Fall Activity – Basketball
31.   Winter Activity – Snowball Fights
32.   Spring Activity – Painting Eggs
33.   Food – Chicken Sandwich
34.   Guitar – ESP Snakebyte
35. Type of weather – Nice Days

Lexi Wright

36 | Well Within Legal Limits

Above you have learned 35 things about me that I hope is somehow useful. Now there is only 11 days until I turn 21.

I don't want to turn 21. I wish we could stay young forever. I'm still not sure what I want to do for my birthday. My 16th birthday, I got an Oreo ice-cream cake and we celebrated at *Frisch's* in Bethel. That was the last celebration of my birthday for some reason. When I turned 17, I can't remember what happened but I know we didn't celebrate my birthday. When I turned 18, we were supposed to go roller skating, but that was turned down. I celebrated my birthday alone that year, pictures on my *Facebook* and in this book. For my 19th birthday, nothing. When I turned 20, we were supposed to go see *Metallica* at *US Bank Arena* but that didn't happen either. So, I won't be surprised if nothing happens this year as well. At least I'll be able to buy my own beer, though. I'm working really hard on this book because I want it to come out awesome. I started writing back in 2016 and it is 2020.

I've been trying to change. I'm talking less, sleeping more, eating less, and even smoking less. We have to hide our cigarettes because we think Dillon might be stealing them while we ain't looking. I hope not. I keep trying to tell him to follow William's path, not mine. I destroyed my life; I don't want him doing the same. The reason I'm changing is because I'm sure nobody likes hearing me talk, I'm sleeping more because that's when I actually feel good, happy for a short while. I'm eating less so that way everyone else can eat and not me. I'm going to quit smoking so that way there are no cigarettes for Dillon to steal from me. It's January 5, 2020, 9 days until I turn 21. I don't even say a word to the dogs anymore. I can't. Roxy has been acting weird lately. She hopped onto to the couch and sat behind me. I didn't say absolutely anything to her whatsoever, I was watching my show on my computer. Well, she started her shaking thing, I move an inch, the more she shook. I was getting irritated, but didn't say anything to her. Because no matter what, I'm the bad person. She finally decides to get down and I was relieved. If I could, I would choose not to have the dogs. I mean, I love them, but they got to stop playing games. I just can't believe that even the dogs hate me. I really think that everyone's life would be better if I wasn't here. Too bad I'm afraid of death. I like to take care of my collection and keep it nice and clean. Every once in a while, I take down my collection, dust off every CD and case, dust off my figurines, then I get a damp washcloth, and carefully wipe down everything. I noticed a couple of my CDs had slight scratches on them, but I'm thinking it's from the CD player, I really don't like it, but what can I do?

One joke that's been going around the family for a while now is, I throw dad in the garbage after beating him up for some reason. Shadow is close to her end, which is making me sad. I told everyone I wanted to be the one to bury her since she was my dog. She's going to be 11 in June, and I heard dogs only live 12 to 15 years. That'd be great if she was immortal. LOL. I'll write more when it gets closer to my birthday.

I'm starting to think that William, Dillon, and Dad all don't like women at all, but know that they have to use them for sex. They have no respect for either me or mom. Mom just talked to me about how dad was treating her last night. And the "My Suspicions" chapter, the things about mom are VERY wrong. Here's what happened: dad calls me into the room basically just to treat me like shit. He asks if I want to split the cigarette, he had in his hand with him or not. But he wouldn't even hand it to me. If I would've tried to take the cigarette, I would've been wrong and gotten yelled at. "Don't snatch the cigarette from me!" or "fine! I'll just quit smoking so that you can have them all!" Something like that. And what I did do was not take it because I was unsure on what to do. And still, wrong for that. I just went back into the living room, sat on the couch, and cried. I tried to cry into my pillow, but he still heard me and had Dillon bring me a cigarette. At that point I was too afraid to smoke, so I gave it back. "From now on don't give her any cigarettes!" I felt like shit. The rest of the night, I tried to go to sleep with no use. Well, mom was getting it now. Dad lays down and goes to sleep after the cigarette fiasco. Mom stayed up and played some games on her phone. After a while, she lays down to go to sleep, well, dad gets up and turns on the light, no respect for mom. He wanted mom to hang out with him and watch movies. It hits 5:30 in the morning and he asks mom if they got paid yet. They didn't get paid till 7. When they did, dad told mom to go to the store and buy cigarettes and gas. Like, why in the entire fuck can't you do it?! All mom wanted to do was sleep and she can't have that. WOW. Mom wants to get a place just for me and her. That'd be great and it'd also suck, because I'm so used to the turmoil and hell, and there won't be any there. At least we'll be able to live, though. But she's too scared to do that because of dad. She's afraid of what dad will do. I don't blame her. But really, what's he going to do? All he'll do is yell at us about it. And? So, I think we should do it. Just get the fuck on up outta here. Women are treated so bad here. Mom gets it, but it seems like me the most. I'm starting to think that maybe the joke about throwing dad in the trash ain't really a joke, like, maybe that's what he wants us to do. We ain't ever going to do it cause we ain't like that, but he thinks I am. Man, I've typed A LOT of words here, huh? Crazy how long it's taking to finish.

Loving James is very, very hard. I feel like a stranger in the family. I hope he reads this book and finally realizes the truth about my love for him. But I'm scared. I love him very much, but I'm scared he'll treat me bad because, well, he's a guy. All guys are the same, I've come to realize that. But maybe, being used to it, I can push through it and still love him. All through my entire life, I've gotten treated like shit from dad, pawpaw, William, Dillon, and when I was younger, Leslie. Sometimes mom treats me bad, but not always. I can see if she doesn't realize, but for the guys? Ha. I'm scared for my future now, because I can see how it turns out for someone whose been treated bad throughout growing up, (ahem, dad). Now, I'm scared to see what the future has in for me. Juuuuust great. ☹

Well, there goes my birthday. I feel like I just caused this to happen because I did good, and when I do good, bad

things happen, well worse things happen. I never brush
my teeth like I should, but I did this morning and mom
and dad were getting ready for work. Well, there's a
knock at the door and it's the people wanting to repo the
car. FUCK! Mom and dad tried everything to keep the
car, but no use. Dads out of work, William can't get back
to school, my birthday is ruined, AGAIN. And we can't
get anywhere for any kind of work whatsoever now. So,
Mom tried calling Chris, dad's friend, to see if he'll either
let us borrow his car or drive us out to Hebron Kentucky
to drop dad off. He said no because he is in the middle of
packing. Guess he found a better place to live. Which is
good because this town fucking sucks. With no luck from
Chris, mom tried talking to pawpaw. Basically, all he said
was, "I don't know what to tell you, Jenny." He's helped,
and helped, and helped, and helped, but he's getting
tired of it. He said in the past that he's going to stop
helping us because it doesn't seem to work. So, with no
luck from Chris or pawpaw, mom and dad are walking to
Family Dollar to see if they are hiring. I hope they are,
because man, we need a job. If they are not hiring, which
I don't think they are, because in the past, I would go
over there and try and get a job. "We're not hiring right
now." or "We're just looking for managers." Or they'll
have a sign up saying they're hiring, but totally ignore my

Lexi Wright

application. So, I'm really hoping they'll play ball with mom and dad and let them have a job in this stink hole you call a town. If they are not hiring, then mom and dad are going over to *Dollar General* and asking them for a job. If *Dollar General* doesn't work out, then they are going to try *Payless Mini Mart*, or just *Payless*. That place I know isn't going to let them work because the owners work there and they only hire teenage girls, or if you're related to them. So, this whole thing fucking sucks! So now how is William supposed to get back to college on Sunday? He has friends that'll give him a ride, but they don't live in this hellhole of a town. They live close to his college. So, I feel bad for William having to figure out a ride situation now that our damn car is gone. Why couldn't they just let us go to work and pay them the stupid money and keep the car? Dad said he wishes mom would just pay the bills, but most of the time, it's just her working and she doesn't make that much. She buys food, cigarettes, and gas, and that's pretty much all she got paid. I want to rob a bank or something to be able to pay bills and everything. But I'm not going to do that. Can't anyway, I'm afraid of people.

So, since my birthday was taken along with the car they reposed, I guess this is all I'm going to write in this chapter. I was really hoping for a good 21st birthday, but you know, whatever. I'm going to go back in time and prevent that life of a so-called childhood. No, but I wish I could. Trust me, if I could go back in time, I'd change A LOT of things, plus, I'd go back to 1981 and go to the *Metallica* studio in California and meet up with James since he'd be 18. I don't really like him in his younger years, I like him more in his older years, but I'd still make him mine right then and there. So now I'm going to play some video games and hope for a better life for when I hit 30. Hopefully.

I said the previous paragraph was it, but more and more shit keeps happening and I want to add some things. First of all, on Tuesday, my birthday, the electric got shut off. So, for 6 days, I've been staying in mom and dad's room trying to stay warm because the house felt like we were living in Antarctica or some shit. The house was dark, completely dark. No sound, nothing. I was afraid to go to sleep because of it being so dark. Finally, I would fall asleep. Once it would get to be about 8 o' clock or so, we'd go over to the walking trail and use the grill and cook up something to eat for dinner. Dad would take one of his knives with him to use on a coyote if one tried to attack. The first night, Dillon went over there with mom and dad and I was left alone. It was creepy. Felt like forever before they showed back up. I went with mom

Lexi Wright

and dad the next night, and Dillon stayed home. Dillon said he already found something to eat, so we just made food for the three of us. We ate at the trail and charged up dad's laptop. When we got back home, we watched a movie until the battery died, then we went to sleep. When we got the electric back on today, which is Monday, I was so happy. I want to add more pictures, which I will do if I find some interesting ones. Right now, I'm listening to *The Dirt* by *Motley Crue*, it's such a good song. I like the chorus: "Just give me the gun! Just give me the gun! Just give me what I want till it hurts! Just give me the gun! Just give me the gun! Let's take it to the top and watch it burn!"

I'm thinking about a couple things. One: get my GED and go to college with William. I wouldn't be in his classes or dorm, but at the same school. I'll major in music and minor in film or video editing. Two: wait till after college to become a rockstar. Maybe it hasn't happened yet because I still need to learn more or something. So, all that talk about me giving up was probably just a slump or I did give up at the moment, but I'm back! Who knows? Maybe Darkness Prevails might rock the world after all, and Lexi Wright will be the best damn rockstar you've ever seen! Watch out world! Darkness Prevails is coming!! You don't really hear too much about people

Starting Things Off Wright

excited to go to school, but I am. I am so excited now. ☺
My dreams could come true after all.

Me, William, and Dillon having fun

Dillon pretending to drive at a car show

In Bethel, Ohio

Dillon acting tough

Our cat, Butterscotch

Lexi Wright

My dad and his Ford F-150 Pickup

My dad also got me interested in guitar

He's playing some *Lynyrd Skynyrd*

Dillon popping a wheelie

July 4th. From right to left, Dad, Dillon

William, Me, Pawpaw, and our neighbor, Juan

Starting Things Off Wright

William's graduation. May 2017

William's HS Diploma

From Left to Right: My Great Aunt Paula, Mom, Me, William

Pawpaw, Dillon, and Dad

Our dog Roxy

Roxy and Kiki

Lexi Wright

Mom and Dad visit

William at his college

At Cincinnati Zoo. Dad, Me, William, and Dillon

I tried to make myself look like

James Hetfield

Me working on some YouTube videos

Starting Things Off Wright

Me in my full 80s heavy metal outfit

A pose I did for my Instagram

I thought I was the biggest rockstar

I thought I was so cool (Still do, ha)

Lexi Wright

37 | Ghostly Evidence

Here are some photos either me or someone in my family has taken. All are paranormal and might scare you.

"Charlette". Photo taken at Smyrna Cemetery, February 1, 2010

Starting Things Off Wright

"3 Headed Indian". Photo taken at an old folk's home, March 7, 2010

"Lady on Tombstone Reading". Photo taken at Felicity Cemetery, May 30, 2009

"Ghost Rider". Photo taken on US 52, from the parking lot of *McDonald's*, March 20, 2012

Lexi Wright

"Knights of Felicity". Photo taken at *Felicity Middle School* parking lot, May 30, 2009

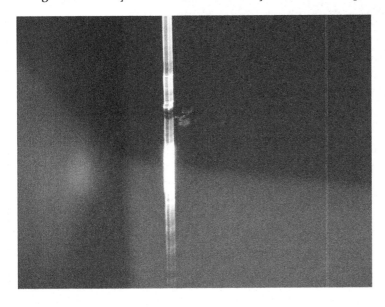

Starting Things Off Wright

"Light Beam". Photo taken in apartment 4 of Felicity Apartments, November 12, 2009

"Woman Head". Photo taken at Felicity Cemetery, March 12, 2010

"Crazy Head Guy". Photo taken at Felicity Soccer/Baseball Field, November 5, 2009

Lexi Wright

Those are just some of the ghost photos I've found. I wish I had photos of the ones I've described in "The Scary Things I've Seen" chapter, except for the first thing I described. I hope you like my book and it comes in handy somehow. Below are some photos I've found of when I was young, also some interesting ones.

June 21, 2009. From right to left, Me, Dillon, Pawpaw, William

November 3, 2009. I always wanted to be in the camera shot for some reason

November 18, 2009. I was 10 years old

Christmas time, December 18, 2009

Starting Things Off Wright

William and Dillon holding Chewy, May 1, 2010

William & Dad's reflection May 30, 2009

William points out a ghost November 7, 2009

Dillon, November 7, 2009

Lexi Wright

Those were all the pictures I could find. I think this book is pretty cool. Whatever I become, a rockstar, author, boxer, whatever it may be, this book will be cool to have, for you to have. Only a limited amount of these are signed or even have my autographed illustration, so some copies may have a blank page, because I drew the illustration by hand, not on computer. There are other books I have started to write, but I think I may just forget those because this one is the only one I really want to write. I've had movie ideas, TV show ideas, but never did anything with them because I don't know how to start a movie, or a TV show. The best TV show idea we ever came up with was *SPI: Society of Paranormal Investigations*. Our motto was, "3 kids, 2 parents, 1 truth". It was going to be like this, I was the lead investigator, William and Dillon were investigators and cameramen, mom and dad were editors and investigators. We were going to go all across the nation searching for the truth. We weren't going to air the episode unless it contained some real evidence, we were never going to fake anything because we wanted to prove the existence of ghosts without trickery or fixed videos. I made a weekly list of what we were going to do each day. Monday, we were going to find our locations. Tuesday, we were going to research our locations to see how haunted it was and what we were going to be dealing with. Wednesday, we were

Starting Things Off Wright

going to film interviews about the location. Thursday, we were going to investigate the location. Friday, we were going to edit the episode and air it on our *YouTube* channel until we did get a TV show. Saturday and Sunday were rest days. It was going to be close to *Ghost Adventures* but with real evidence and nothing fake at all. And only a few episodes aired because we mostly wouldn't catch anything. We didn't do the show because we didn't want any problems with ghosts. We didn't want them following us home, scratching us, or harming us in any way, plus we were afraid of what we might catch on either film or photo, mostly evp, electronic voice phenomena. One thing I wish we did have on film was the military guy me and Dillon saw at a World War 2 cemetery. It was broad daylight and we just walk in to the cemetery. I happen to look up from my camera and at the far end of the cemetery I saw a man dressed in army clothes completely see-through walk towards a tree and never come out the other side. It didn't scare me, it surprised me. As we were leaving, we told the ghosts, "get ready for us, cause we're coming back tonight." We shouldn't have said that or returned because we got some activity. I think me and Dillon were trying to film episode one of *SPI*, can't remember. But we got spooky pictures and a voice saying, "wrong person" in a whisper. The vibe was not good there at all either. As we left, we

Lexi Wright

both heard a little girl singing, "la-la-la-la-la-la", Dillon looked back and he said he saw two eyes and a black figure at the entrance of the graveyard. So, we hustled on our bikes out of there as fast as we could. That was the last time we ghost hunted because, as it turned out, things followed us home. We began having troubles with seeing things, things moving on their own, hearing voices and scary noises. We moved out and haven't had paranormal issues since. Which is good. I think we learned our lesson there.

The back of my Battle Jacket.

Started June 2019, finished November 2020

The right side

The left side

My bullet belt

Starting Things Off Wright

So much stuff has happened over the last 21 years. When I first thought about writing this book, I never thought I'd get this far. I thought it would be an Encyclopedia sized book with every single thing that has happened until the day I turned 80 or so. But, I figured, this is enough and it is the best book I have ever written. So, more and more things will continue to go on, maybe I'll write a sequel, I don't know. We'll have to see how life goes.

And so, this is everything I wanted to add. What a story to tell. Remember to make the wright choices! Welcome to the year 2020, the so-called future.

I hope you enjoyed my book; it is completely about my whole life, up until now, January 21, 2020. I hope you find inspiration and hope through my life, and I hope to influence readers to do what's right, and find what's right for them. And don't forget, Always Make The Wright Choices!

About The Author

What could be said here? This is all about Lexi Wright, the author. 21 years old, a near-successful YouTuber, a Musician, and a daughter/sister to a wonderful family. Read this book to learn more about the author which is said about in this whole story of life once known.

Starting Things Off Wright

Acknowledgments

Thank you to everyone who have helped me create this amazing story and who have helped me throughout life.

Everyone in my family:

Don Sack, Donald Sack III, Jennifer Sack, William Sack, Dillon Sack, Paula Sack – Strudevent.

And James Hetfield (*Metallica*).

Friends:

Chris McDonald, Tami Bremer, Jazalyn Santel.

I'd also like to thank the staff at *James Saul's Homeless Shelter* in Batavia, Ohio.

I'd like to thank *Microsoft*, because without them, I would never have been able to write this book with so much ease on my laptop, with *Windows 10*.

(*Any asterisks in the book signify a fantasy I wished would happen but I didn't explain it was a fantasy in writing. *)

Lexi Wright

Life can be hard, and Lexi Wright knows that. Follow alongside her as she tells the story of how success can be found, through hell and back again. Take a trip inside her mind and find out some things you may not have known about Lexi Wright. Also, a very special someone has been mentioned quite a lot in this book, guess who? Hint: he's the frontman, singer, and guitarist of the biggest metal band in history, since 1981. So, before you go thinking your life sucks, read this interesting story to see if you can relate to some of the things Lexi talks about. From birth to age 21, she explains in deep detail every aspect of her life, good and bad. She also explains the hardships of achieving your dreams, be it whatever you wish. Lexi explains the true horrors of depression, the frightening truth of the paranormal, and the difference between true love and fake love. Find out what you thought you knew about Lexi Wright and you may be blown away to what you might learn. Enjoy this trip of informative, historical, and frightening events that occur between 1999 and 2020. What could you learn?

Made in the USA
Columbia, SC
20 July 2022

63662520R00095